T0354739

TWICE
COLOMBIA

Adventure, Friendship, *and*
Adoption *in the*
Andes Mountains

Patricia L. Woodard

Order this book online at www.trafford.com
or email orders@trafford.com

Most Trafford titles are also available at major online book retailers.

Print information available on the last page.

ISBN: 978-1-6987-1645-9 (sc)
ISBN: 978-1-6987-1646-6 (e)

Library of Congress Control Number: 2024903169

Trafford rev. 04/17/2024

   www.trafford.com
North America & international
toll-free: 844-688-6899 (USA & Canada)
fax: 812 355 4082

In memory of Jamie, my sweet prince,
and my incredible parents.

Author's Note

The characters who enriched this memoir are real. In a few
cases I changed their names to protect their privacy. My
interpretation of Latin American politics is based on what I
observed while living in Colombia and may or may not be
historically accurate. My intention was to set the stage.

References

Prochnau, William. "Adventures in the Ransom Trade." *Vanity Fair,* May, 1998, pp.134-158.

Lefson, Neill and Peter C. Keller. "How an earthquake brought to light the opulent treasure of Popayan." Pp.139-146. Magazine unknown. (Accent needed on the second a in Popayan)

Books By Patricia L. Woodard

Twice Colombia
Dos Veces en Colombia
We're Waiting on You
Ava and Salomé – Welcome to Cali!

Table of Contents

Author's Note vii
References ix

PART ONE—BOGOTÁ

The Telegram 1
Orientation In Miami 5
Arrival In Bogotá 9
Moving In 22
A Final Fling 26
The Students Arrive 30
Roommates And Becoming Southern 32
The Red Ruana And First Date 38
Demonstrations And Omar Shariff 46
Melgar And The National Pastime 51
Tight Underwear And The President's Palace 56
Hospital Trip 61
Custom-Made Cape 66
First Party And Thanksgiving 71
Cousin Dave And The Women 76
Home For The Holidays 80
New Years Holiday In San Andres 83
Medical Emergency 87
A Lost Month 91
¡Ciao, Colombia! 93
Transition 105
¡Bienvenido! 107

PART TWO—CALI

    Another Opportunity...127

    Happy Birthday!...129

    New Apartment, New Roommates 131

    Popayan And South Pacific.......................................137

    Chiquitines 141

    Bombs, Explosions And How To Mail Cheese 146

    Boy Or Girl?..150

    Mom's Visit 155

AUGUST 1984 – JUNE 1985

    August 1984..169

    September 1984 173

    October 1984 176

    November 1984..182

    December 1984..190

    January 1985..197

    February 1985...201

    March 1985 209

    April 1985..212

    May 1985 215

    June 1985 220

Mission Accomplished..225

Epilogue 227

PART ONE

Bogotá

The Telegram

The day the telegram arrived I was as complacent as all the other
days that summer. The sun was bright, the humidity was abundant,
and the arrival of afternoon rain was just a matter of time. The day
was about as ordinary as it gets in southeastern North Carolina, and
my wanderlust and need for new pursuits were in check. I tell you
this because these two forces that had motivated my actions for a
long time were soon to be reawakened.

In the summer of 1975 I was teaching math at Whiteville High
School to a group of students who had failed algebra 1 or geometry
the previous year. What was a death sentence for some teachers
was for me a great way to spend part of my vacation. Summer
school was always more relaxing and in many ways more rewarding
than the regular term. Most of the students were motivated; they
needed to get credit for failed classes, and with smaller class sizes

1

I could develop closer relationships and spend more time with each one individually. They responded to the attention and were nearly always successful. That summer was a good time, too, for me professionally, and I was content with my efforts. Ready to begin my third year at the same school as chairman of the Mathematics Department, I faced new challenges as Segregation was slowly coming to an end in the public schools of southeastern North Carolina.

I had nearly forgotten about an application I had filed with a school in Bogotá, Colombia, a few months earlier, especially since the initial correspondence from the school said there was no math vacancy for the coming year. They would keep my application on file, however, and contact me if an opening occurred. Okay. I knew the routine, and I tucked away that endeavor. At some point I would try again for another job overseas if this one didn't work out, and that was fine with me. Living and working in a foreign culture had always been a dream, but South America had not been my first choice, so a rejection from a school in Colombia didn't seem significant. What could be so appealing about Colombia, anyway? The country had the drug trade and violence and earthquakes, but what else?

And then, that sultry afternoon in late June, I was unwinding from a good workday when the doorbell rang, and there stood a man from Western Union with a telegram. It said:

OFFER SEVENTH EIGHTH GRADE MATHEMATICS STOP YEARLY SALARY PLUS GRANT TOTAL 8.141 STOP REPLY BY JULY TWO BY CABLE COLEGIO NUEVA GRANADA CARRERA SEGUNDA ESTE NUMERO 70-2# BOGOTÁ COLOMBIA

PHYLLIS MULLENAX DIRECTOR

Stunned, incredulous, I stared at the telegram, ran through all the implications and tried to absorb the shock of seeing an elusive dream reappear and come within such close reach. I nearly exploded with insane laughter. Was I finally getting this offer after so many years of wanting to live and work overseas? Did I really want to leave home? What did I know about Bogotá, or Colombia, for that matter? It was the end of June, and if I accepted their offer, I would be leaving in August. Would I have enough time to close up my house, sell my car, and take care of the endless details involved in moving to a foreign country? It didn't take long for those feelings of adventure and longing to reappear, or for me to decide. After calling my parents and a few friends, and thinking about how I would tell my principal I wouldn't be back next year, I sent a telegram to Phyllis Mullenax, Director. Yes, I could accept and yes, the time was right.

The following weeks came to life with urgency as information from CNG arrived with detailed instructions for preparing for the move. Always a list maker, I now kept a running to-do list on a legal pad and never tore a page off for fear of forgetting something monumental. What furniture I couldn't sell I donated or put in storage at my patient and generous parents' house. I moved in with them after clearing out my own house and took over two rooms where I sorted clothes - those to take with me and those to store. I identified household items I would need and put aside a few school supplies I thought I could use anywhere in the world. I scheduled medical and dental appointments and immunization shots. A letter from the local police department stated that I was a citizen in good standing. The details were endless, but gradually the dream was all coming together. I watched my "to-do" list get smaller and smaller, while my anticipation and curiosity grew stronger and stronger.

For the last few weeks of summer school I struggled to stay grounded, and, gratefully, the time passed quickly. After exams I cleaned out my classroom. Whiteville High School had been good to me, and, in time, some of the fondest memories of my career would center on the two years I spent there.

With school out I had time to take care of the final details and pack up household items I was allowed to ship separately. Sheets, blankets, towels, extension cords, blender and several small kitchen appliances were all in those boxes. I also packed feminine hygiene products, special shampoos and conditioners just for blondes. For clothes, the school advised us to bring things that could be layered but to leave heavy winter clothes at home. So, sweaters, blazers, hose, socks and underwear filled up the nooks and crannies of the boxes, protecting the bottles of make-up, perfume and other toiletry items. CNG hinted that we might receive our boxes soon after we arrived. The Department of Security Administration, (DAS), similar to our FBI, had to inspect the boxes and, at the time, I just assumed the boxes would all be at the school when I arrived. I was not too concerned about when I would see them again.

A friend bought my car and took care of the title transfer and other details. He graciously agreed to let me keep it until I left and in so doing allowed me the means to tackle the last surge of activity without having to borrow my parents' cars. Always supportive of this adventure, he was a steady and dependable friend.

The night before I left, my sister Sara and her four young children prepared a farewell party at her house. Her oldest daughter, Shannon, then eleven years old, baked and decorated a cake with red, yellow, and blue icing depicting the Colombian flag. Friends and family took pictures and we ate good food. I felt secure in knowing that my support system was in place. I knew that I was headed toward something mysterious and magical, but, exactly what, I wasn't sure, and I could barely contain my excitement.

And finally, at 5 a.m., August 13, 1975, my parents and I left Whiteville for the one-hour trip to the Wilmington airport. I checked two suitcases and carried a pocketbook, a raincoat, a couple of books and plenty of Dramamine to ease the flight through the turbulent winds over the Andes. As I walked across the tarmac and waved to my parents, a searing image burned in my mind of the two of them standing there. For the only time in this entire adventure, while I blew a goodbye kiss in their direction, I had a very childlike feeling of separation anxiety, and wondered what I had gotten myself into.

Orientation In Miami

On the flight to Miami for the orientation, I had time to finish one of the books on the recommended reading list, *One Hundred Years of Solitude*, by the Colombian writer Gabriel García Márquez. As I closed the covers and daydreamed, my imagination entered his world of magical realism, and I wondered how the pursuit of this new adventure would enrich my life.

We met for a four-day orientation at the storied Fontainbleu Hotel in Miami Beach (where Sean Connery had filmed scenes for the movie *Goldfinger*). The new import teachers, (that's what those of us from places other than Colombia were called), gathered to hear from people associated with the school and to meet each other. There were also new teachers from the nine other bilingual and multicultural schools in Colombia which were accredited by the Southern Association of Colleges and Schools. Experts would be there to help prepare all of us for the culture shock we could expect.

When I checked into my room and noticed that the price of one night was $50, I was greatly relieved that the school paid for this part of the trip. They would house us, feed us and care for all of our needs while in Miami and, in fact, until we were settled in our apartments in Bogotá. A teacher from New Hampshire, Sarah, and I shared a room for the four nights in Miami, and I was anxious about the idea of having roommates again. After all, I was thirty-one years old, had lived on my own for several years, and wasn't sure I could share space with a roommate again as I had done in college. Doing that would be an adjustment for me, but the desire to have the experience in Colombia required that I be flexible and open and remember the objectives, so I tried not to let my desire for privacy be a concern.

When Sarah arrived, we both quickly realized that our goals were similar and that we had a lot in common. Of course! *All* of us shared similar goals. Otherwise, why would we be headed to a plateau high in the Andes Mountains in South America for a year? The tumultuous period of the late sixties and early seventies in the United States had profoundly affected our personal lives, and we were open to new challenges. As opportunity and change again came our way, the pursuit of this adventure seemed a proper next step in our search for self-fulfillment. Whatever it was that led us to undertake this trip was not easy to identify.

"I'm looking for a new adventure," said Sarah, "and I need some time to think about my relationship with my boyfriend. I'm not sure I want to get married right now, and I was beginning to feel some pressure to make a decision."

"I understand completely. Sometimes a little distance can be a good thing for a relationship. I guess I'm here because I've always had an interest in foreign cultures and know so little about South America. I thought it would be a good way to experience the culture first hand," I said. "Also, I want to work on my Spanish, and, to be honest, I'm curious about this country."

Sarah and I developed an easy rapport quickly. In the days to come, as all of us discussed our reasons, our restlessness, and tossed around ideas, we gradually accepted that maybe we didn't know exactly why we thought this venture would be productive for us. But the one thing we all agreed on was that it was a quest for something we weren't finding in our lives at home. The members of our group seemed compatible, and as we looked at each other, talked and shared meals, we formed bonds that, even in the short time we spent together in Miami, seemed strong.

In our group there were two married couples, and eight of us were single. Of the single group, there were three males and five females. As far as I could tell, we were all within five years of being thirty. One of the couples, Doug and Martha, brought along three young children, and the other couple, Bruce and Movelle, fellow Southerners, were newlyweds. We came with varied experiences and from different backgrounds. Barb from Pennsylvania had taught in Venezuela, and the rest of us had spent time in schools all over the United States. All of us had left behind past relationships, and most of us had left a current boyfriend or girlfriend at home. There was one divorcee, Denise, and the rest of us had teetered around the marriage issue with three broken engagements among us, mine included. We were from rural areas, small towns and large cities, different religions and different heritages. The melting pot in the United States was represented here in our group, and we would learn a lot about different cultures from within our own ranks.

During the workshops we heard from import teachers who had already spent a few years at the school. We listened to their experiences with housing, maids, dealing with students and parents from all over the world, getting around the city, dating within the local community, crime and safety concerns, and third-world politics. An entire afternoon detailed security issues and the very real threats to Americans living in Bogotá. We were led to believe that we, individually, were not likely to be targets for political kidnappings because we probably would not generate the ransom that fueled the guerilla and terrorist groups. Our students, however, many of whom were children of embassy personnel or high-ranking Colombian government officials, had, in fact, been targets. Because of our proximity to them, we were vulnerable, too. It would be crucial for us to be vigilant. The high crime rate, which we were all familiar with, had its roots in the poor economy and, as foreigners, we were definitely in a high-risk group and subject to harm. Anything we could do to appear inconspicuous would be to our advantage. We heard warnings about the severe consequences of being caught with drugs and horror stories about Colombian jails. Also, it was not out of the question that we might have to evacuate the city following some crisis, and we received full instructions on how to proceed should that ever become necessary. That crisis presentation continued for a long time and made a big impact on all of us and was a sobering reminder that we were not on vacation. The beginning of an uneasiness that never let up started with that workshop and touched every aspect of our lives for the entire time in Colombia.

Another workshop dealt with reverse culture shock. All of us had signed a one-year contract, and many would be returning after that time to the States. A few would extend their contracts in Bogotá, some would go to other schools in South America or Europe, and others would return home. I don't think anyone had given a second thought to adjustment concerns when our year was over. That discussion was one of the most valuable of the entire orientation. The cultural information was useful in phone calls when we tried to make small talk with our families back home and also on special occasions when friends or family came to visit. Our relationships with those we left behind would change, and sometimes, we were told, we'd feel like strangers in our most familiar surroundings. In essence, we would have this immense personal experience that would impact our lives forever, but the people closest to us back home, while they would probably have interest, would be living their own lives and would never ask more than a few questions about what we had been through. Fair enough. This endeavor was simply an individual choice for each of us. So, I came to understand, before ever arriving in Bogotá, that my year would be a private affair and not something to be shared easily. At home, those people who really wanted to know what life was like would make an effort to ask questions. Most people really wouldn't care, and I was okay with that. The message? Don't expect others automatically to share your enthusiasm about this experience.

The workshop was thorough and the consultants were well qualified. By the last night in Miami I had already learned more about the Colombian culture than I thought possible and was eager to move on to the next level. We were leaving early the next morning for Bogotá, and in the next few days we would decide on living arrangements, roommates, and see the school and city for the first time. I was thrilled.

Arrival In Bogotá

When my sister Rachel found out I had accepted a teaching position in a private school in Bogotá, well known as the drug capital of the world, she said all she could visualize about Colombia were women with baskets on their heads. Although I had read every book on the recommended reading list for the import teachers, I'll admit that I also shared that romantic vision: native women with dark glistening skin, balancing those huge fruit baskets, with yards and yards of cotton skirts swirling around their bare feet. Smiling, happy faces, and strolling in the sunshine down a narrow, dirt path with banana trees and coffee bushes shading their trail. Oh, yes, I knew it was a fantasy but it was a real image I had carried for a long time.

The flight on the Colombian airline, Avianca, from Miami to Bogotá, presented a truer picture of Colombia and its people. The plane was full of people who seemed to be Colombian, who were dressed just as we were, and who were engaged in the same things we were doing: reading, eating, drinking and chatting quietly with their companions. Whenever there was a jolt or sudden change in altitude, they closed their eyes and crossed themselves. This gesture was a reminder that 95 percent of Colombians were Catholic and that my Protestant background would put me in the minority, although I never hesitated to cross myself when I needed reassurance and hoped I wasn't being blasphemous. The in-flight service, food, drinks and camaraderie were superb and plentiful, and my confidence in the Colombian airline was strong. Flying over the Andes was turbulent, but the view, when there was a view, was magnificent. Just the thought of being where I was at that particular time was thrilling.

We landed on schedule at the bustling and sprawling El Dorado airport in Bogotá. With the help of officials from the school we passed through Customs and Immigration with few problems, other than the endless waiting. I learned a new word that day, "*palanca*," which means "influence or pull," and thank God we had some of that. It was one of those unsettling concepts that I struggled with for a long time. Since our bags were checked quickly and nothing was confiscated, it was obvious the school had connections with the right people.

As I looked around the airport and took in the smells, the sounds, and the people, the one thing I didn't see was women with fruit baskets on their heads. I was visually jolted by the cosmopolitan and sophisticated people: the men with their aura of healthy pride and the women, in particular, who wore their aristocratic bearing in the same way they wore their smooth and chocolatey-textured leather boots, their professionally styled hairdos and their plush, soft, woolen ruanas – confidently and comfortably. It was exciting to be surrounded by this new environment and even the exhaustion of a long day didn't dampen my enthusiasm.

We arrived at our hotel late in the afternoon, and after getting settled in the European-style pension, sharing bathrooms and being assigned three to a room, we stumbled down to our first Colombian dinner. The hotel provided breakfast and dinner until we found our own housing, and we ate whatever they served us. That first dinner was typical of basic Colombian fare: steak (no one seemed to know what cut), rice, potatoes, salad, and dessert. Personally, I had very little appetite that evening, and after only a few bites, my head started swimming, and I decided to leave the dining room. I made it as far as the parlor before collapsing on the sofa. The next thing I remembered was a hotel employee leaning over me, saying, "*Tranquila*. It's the altitude. Food cools off fast, women gain weight, and most people get sick when they come here the first time. So just rest and try to get some sleep. You'll feel better tomorrow."

And so, with reassurance and relief that it wasn't just the free wine we indulged in on the flight down, I made it upstairs, with the help of Jerry from Arizona, and Barb, who was becoming a close companion, and yielded to the storied altitude and its effect on nearly everything. In time, we came to blame everything that went wrong on the altitude, especially when it was convenient to have a scapegoat. That night, however, I didn't question the altitude, only my judgment in deciding to commit to a year here.

I later found out that I wasn't the only one who got sick the first night, and I'm glad to say it was my one and only experience with altitude sickness. Coming from coastal Carolina to an altitude of 8,661 feet was a staggering jolt to my system, but strong and healthy, I took only a day to get my bearings again.

After a fitful night with sleep coming begrudgingly, I awoke surprisingly refreshed and re-energized. We made our way to the dining room and devoured scrambled eggs, a delicious and light, buttery puff of bread called *pan de bono*, fresh pineapple, and the justly famous Colombian coffee. As my colleagues drifted in, I began to hear mumbling about their cold showers, skimpy towels, and uncomfortable beds. Apparently, the hotel had a limited amount of hot water, and those who showered last were left with nothing but icy sprays. The water pressure, too, was iffy. None too pleasant an ordeal when the temperature was 48 degrees, the air was damp, and there was no heat in the rooms.

Most of the females had their own towels, but none of the guys had thought about putting at least one in their suitcases and asked to borrow from us. It was the first time I'd ever shared a towel with a male who wasn't my boyfriend, and after I gladly loaned one to Jerry, the Linda Ronstadt-loving guy from Arizona, he and I became great friends. We all figured out pretty quickly that as long as we were in the hotel we'd have to make a schedule to ensure hot showers for everyone. And so we did.

Before starting the hunt for housing, we rode a bus to the government agency called DAS to be fingerprinted, photographed, and otherwise identified. After a few hours in a small, dark room with unsteady, metal shelves full of ancient folders seemingly stacked haphazardly and reaching to the ceiling, we finally received papers allowing us to work and live in Colombia. While waiting, most of us opted to let the other applicants have the few chairs. We sat on the floor, smoked and drank *tinto*, small cups of strong espresso-type coffee sweetened heavily with sugar. We were still tired, riding on a caffeine high. It was a rainy day, bleak, mid 50s; the wind, at times, especially when doors opened and closed, was ferocious. In the next year we endured many dealings with DAS, and I always remembered vividly that first day amid the stacks of folders, tired employees, and drinking coffee sitting on the floor. Bogotá's bureaucracy was so different from how I imagined Federal offices in Washington, D.C. Although I did make comparisons frequently in the beginning, before long tedium became the norm, and I rarely thought about it. Bureaucracy was bureaucracy in any environ.

The next day we encountered the banking system, opened checking accounts, and exchanged dollars for pesos. The bank required cash to open an account, and we were skeptical when they didn't give us receipts immediately. The rep from the school, however, assured us this was normal, and there was nothing to worry about. And, sure enough, the next day someone brought us our receipts and a book of checks, and we had a session on how to write checks. We would end up doing most of our banking at school, where we could write checks and get cash. When the time came later for us to buy dollars instead of pesos, the school did the exchange. All of our financial transactions between the States and Bogotá, in fact, were processed through the school.

From the bank our guides took us to a local, government-operated co-op where we bought *ruanas*, the woolen poncho-type coats which everybody wore and were so perfect for the weather. They were not water repellent, but somehow managed to protect from the cold rain and wind. Made of 100 percent wool, there were short ones and long ones, all heavy and soft. Most of the colors were in neutral, earthy tones-tan, brown, gray and a deep burgundy. There were a few that had stripes, but most were solid colors. A bright red one caught my eye, and I immediately chose it, clueless about the unwanted attention a blond *gringa* in a red coat would garner among a sea of brunettes in neutral. But it was luxurious and beautiful and full length and, at the time, I thought it was perfect. So much for the school's advice to remain inconspicuous. These ruanas also served as blankets until our household goods arrived, and we treasured them.

The next shopping stop was a leather store where we bought backpacks. Since we'd be doing a lot of walking and climbing in the city and at school, we needed the support of a sturdy backpack. Anything to make life more comfortable for us seemed to be the theme of the day, and we didn't hesitate to invest in good quality bags. While there, we also admired luxurious handbags and boots and later returned to add more leather to our wardrobes.

That night the hotel was a welcome respite, and we relaxed at dinner with more steak, rice, potatoes, and salad. Soup was added to our meal and soon became a much-anticipated course. The one we were served that night was hot, tasty and filling. Someone identified cilantro as one of the herbs used in everything we ate, and we could only guess at the other seasonings. And what kind of beans were these? Garbanzos? Navy beans? Whatever they were, they were simmered and cooked into a thick, rich, and comforting dish. And I had never liked beans. Our meal stretched out for nearly two hours as we talked about our day and sipped Chilean wine. By the time we finished all we wanted to do was sleep. Tomorrow we'd finally start looking for housing.

"Look for a sign that says '*Se Arrienda*'- For Rent, or 'Se Vende'-For Sale. Sometimes apartments advertised for sale can be rented, so look for both."

Our driver that day was Rosemarie, an English lady who had two children at CNG. Her husband was connected to the Embassy, and this was their third year in Bogotá. Several parents had volunteered to help us navigate the city, driving through acceptable neighborhoods and pointing out features we needed to think about in choosing living quarters. These ladies went beyond the call of duty as they fought the traffic, found parking places, and served as intermediaries between the maids who stayed in the apartments and our overwhelmed group of four appreciative expats.

"*Podemos ver el apartamento?*" "Can we see the apartment?" There was no way we could not pick up expressions like that as we waited for the maids to unlock the countless doors and let us in. If there was some resistance, Rosemarie would explain that she was with "*professores del Colegio Nueva Granada,*" teachers from Colegio Nueva Granada. That must have carried some weight because we gained entry to every place where we stopped. Our

Spanish was improving quickly as we listened to the exchanges between Rosemarie and the maids.

By the end of the day we still had not found anything suitable, but we knew how to say in Spanish, "Can we see the apartment?" Graciously, Rosemarie said we would try again the next day and that we should not be discouraged. Tired and wanting to empty our suitcases and get settled, we were determined to find something soon even if it meant splitting up.

My friend Jerry, the Art teacher Ellen, the Science teacher Matthew, and I were hoping to find an apartment large enough for all of us, but we couldn't find anything with four bedrooms, in a good location in our price range. There were available houses, but renting houses was complicated so we agreed to divide up if we couldn't find something the next day. Once we made that decision, we were able to settle on things quickly. Ellen and I found a three-bedroom apartment with maid's quarters close to a small shopping center, and Jerry and Matt found a smaller, two- bedroom basement apartment that suited them fine. Our places were only two blocks apart, and I was happy to know that friends would be close by. With that decision made, the school took over the paper work and arranged for utilities. When Rosemarie bid farewell, we were impressed with the assistance the school had provided. They had made quite a financial investment just to get us here and didn't want to risk losing anybody before school even started, so they became our provider and caretaker. I couldn't imagine trying to find my own housing and dealing with the paperwork in a foreign country with only the smattering of language skills I had at the time. In spite of thinking of ourselves as independent, adventurous souls, we knew how much we needed the school's help and were grateful.

With all of us quickly finding apartments or rooms, we soon were able to venture out in the city without school personnel while waiting for our moving dates. We rode the buses and found out which ones to stay away from. We mostly moved around in groups of three or four and felt safe, but we avoided *el centro*, the downtown area, because of the high crime rate there. We practiced our Spanish in restaurants and stores and laughed a lot when no one understood us.

The weather was delightful for the next few days. Brisk, refreshing and stimulating but not cold - is the way it was when the sun was out, but the rainy season, with its 54-degree average temperature, could be rather bleak, like our first day at DAS. Since Bogotá is just 4 degrees north of the Equator, there's very little change in temperature during the year and only two seasons-- rainy and not. But these early days were perfect, and I couldn't help but wonder how I ever survived in tropical southeastern North Carolina. Then I remembered that the hot, humid weather back home didn't last all year and that each change of season there brought renewal and inspiration. I remembered summer days that often stretched into 9 p.m. and winter evenings that ended abruptly at 5 p.m. Now I'd have a chance to live in a climate that rarely changed through the year, where sunset was at 6 p.m. and sunrise at 6 a.m. all year, and I was curious about how I would adapt.

We soon had a chance to enjoy the outdoors even more when we were invited to the *finca* - a vacation house outside the city - belonging to Dr. Mullenax, the Director of CNG. She insisted that we call her Phyllis and somewhat reluctantly we did. I could only think about calling Mr. Mayo, the superintendent of Craven County Schools where I had worked for six years, Hiram, and knew I could never have done that. Was this kind of familiarity typical of the culture, or was it just unique to this job? Whatever the explanation, there was definitely a difference in my previous work environments and this one.

The finca itself was high in the mountains, and the school bus that took us there struggled when shifting gears and kicking gravel into motion. Sunday is the traditional Colombian family day, and this day was glorious, sunny and cold. As we ascended the mountain, the pollution and noise of the city quickly disappeared. Emissions controls on motor vehicles had not yet come to Colombia. When the finca came into view amid the dense forest, it captivated us. The house itself, small and unpretentious, was nestled in a pocket of lush farmland. A brook meandered around the side of the house and through the trees in the front yard, and horses and burros grazed in a nearby pasture. There was a small soccer field (the favorite national sport) and a luxurious carpet of emerald green grass. The only things that seemed out of place were the two guards at the gate, each wearing a machete on one hip and carrying firearms on the other. I couldn't help staring at these men; I couldn't imagine living in a country where guards and firearms were such an overt part of daily life. But, of course, that's exactly what I was doing.

We had been told to pack a lunch, so after about an hour we put our ruanas on the ground and delved into our backpacks. We had picked up sandwiches, chips, fruit and cookies at the grocery store before leaving, all of which tasted wonderful. Phyllis provided beer and cokes, so we had everything we needed. We went in her house only to use the bathroom, and I truly don't recall anything about the interior other than the maid, who was just a very quiet presence showing us where to go. She was the wife of one of the guards, and she and her husband took care of the property for Phyllis. Later, after visiting many fincas, I realized that decorations and home furnishings mattered only in providing the basic comforts. What seemed to matter was that the owners and their friends could enjoy a reprieve from a tense and fearful existence in a politically charged urban atmosphere. With armed guards at the fincas, I wondered how safe they really felt.

After lunch we took siestas under Carolina Blue skies and then strolled around the finca's property. Jerry, Matt, Barb, and Phyllis' son Tony took part in a pick-up soccer game.

"I'll watch, my food needs to settle," I said to Jerry when he asked me to join. In fact, I didn't know anything about soccer.

As the day stretched into late afternoon, we packed up and headed back down the mountain. If a day at the finca was a Colombian custom, then I was grateful to become a part of it. It was thrilling and comforting to be with colleagues I liked, to enjoy simple and good food, to relax in a low-key atmosphere and to relish the pristine beauty of this setting away from the city. When I remember that day, I can feel the warmth of the sun and the frigid air of the mountains. It was a perfect combination and typical of the many contrasts I would encounter in Colombia. Halcyon days indeed.

With moving day fast approaching, we went shopping again, but this time for toilet paper, plates and cups, silverware, detergent, and plastic containers for our school lunches. We also picked up nonperishable staples, such as coffee, salt and pepper, and sugar. Our plan was to shop for food daily until we could furnish our kitchen and hire a maid. We had no word about when our household goods might arrive, but they would probably not be here by the time we moved. We would be living for a while without the luxury of sheets and pillows, pots and pans, and all of those things we so carefully chose to pack in our airfreight. It just didn't seem to be much of a problem then, however, as we were learning to get along with very little. Until we actually moved in, we wouldn't know exactly what we needed so we kept our shopping lists short.

Before the new, import teachers moved out of the hotel into our new apartments, the school arranged a welcoming reception on campus. The plan was for us to look around, meet the principals and support staff, and visit our classrooms.

So, after nine days in Colombia we climbed onto the bus again to travel as a group through the city, quietly taking in the sights. Parts were becoming familiar now and not so strange; the donkey being led down a city street barely warranted a second glance and we expected the beggars on street corners. The children - there seemed to be so many - dressed in rags with cardboard shoes tied with string, were the most difficult to accept. With one look into their eyes, I sensed despair, poverty and abandonment, and as often as not, they met my eyes with a heartbreaking smile. I never got used to seeing so many of them in such great need. There seemed to be more police on the streets with each passing day, and the sight of them with their automatic weapons disturbed me. The police here in the city were the military police, and their uniforms were fatigues rather than smartly tailored navy-blue suits. I was beginning to think of the government and the military in Colombia as the same entity. As we settled in for the cross-city ride, Denise mentioned a story in the newspaper that morning about a worldwide Witches' Conference being held in Bogotá with more than two thousand witches from all over the world in attendance. The implications were obvious. After all, *we* had just gathered in Bogotá, and as we rumbled through the city we laughed when we imagined the reactions of our family and friends (and maybe former students?) if the Witches Conference made the News back home.

After nearly thirty minutes the bus reached the edge of the plateau in the northern part of the city where the upper classes lived, and we headed up the mountain to the school. We wondered about the condition of these old buses on the treacherous roads and hairpin curves and held our breath when the road seemed to disappear. The bus driver told us that the best mechanics in the world lived in Colombia, and we needn't worry. To keep these old buses from the States in good working order, they *had* to be good mechanics.

Surrounding the campus was a twelve-foot electronic fence. The guards on duty opened the gate for our bus; guards were posted twenty-four hours a day, and dogs patrolled at night for extra security. There were three distinct levels of buildings for lower, middle, and upper schools--all surrounding a center for offices, dining facilities, and library. The gymnasium was off to the right, and several smaller structures were scattered around. Everything seemed tucked into a crevice in the mountain. The levels were connected by stone terraces and steep, nearly vertical steps. Beautifully landscaped grounds with splashes of pink, purple, white and yellow filled the school yard. Gardeners kept working diligently. I recognized impatiens amid well-tended shrubbery and trees that I wasn't familiar with. Benches beckoned. Though the sun was shining brightly that day, as the wind whipped around the campus, we snuggled into our ruanas even more tightly as we walked to the welcoming center.

Phyllis, the Director, met us and quickly introduced us to the three principals - one for each school. My principal was Terry, a North American married to a Colombian woman, who was also a teacher. He had smooth, shiny red hair and two noticeably arched eyebrows. The other two principals were from the States, as well, with wives who also worked at CNG. Most of the guidance counselors, nurses and secretaries were Colombian and spoke English as they welcomed us. When Phyllis got up to speak, she addressed her remarks to us, the teachers.

"You're all here because the board felt that you had the professional qualities and skills necessary to support the goals of our school. Your references, your experience, your interview, and your individual achievements indicate that you share our vision of excellence as we prepare our students for the world beyond CNG. Your eagerness to accept new challenges will take you far. You will bring your own stamp to our programs, and we look forward to it and will learn from you. So, thank you for your dedication, and we look forward to a productive year."

I quietly reflected on her comments and thought about the successes I had had in the classroom. I hoped I would have something unique to contribute and that I could provide the support my students needed. That was where my special talents lay – establishing expectations and helping students meet those expectations. There was no greater reward for a teacher than watching a student grow and knowing you had some influence.

We met a few more people. There was a man who spoke no English whose job was to handle all copying tasks. That would be a pleasant change from U.S. schools. Having somebody else in charge of that time-consuming chore, even if we had very limited quotas for paper, was going to be a great time saver. To communicate with him, we filled out forms before submitting requests.

And then there was dignified Doña Vargas, head of the Bachillerato program, who watched over the Colombian Ministry's strenuous requirements for high school graduation. She was the school's main liaison with the government whenever a liaison was needed.

As Phyllis introduced me to each person, I started hearing, "Hello, Pot, welcome," "Hello, Pot, I'm very happy to meet you," "Pot, if there's anything I can do for you, let me know."

Pot? I realized very quickly that I didn't want to be known as "Pot" and immediately started using my given name, "Patricia," not shortened in Colombia to "Pat" or "Pot." It took a while to convince my fellow teachers to call me "Patricia," but eventually they did and that's who I became.

After introductions we enjoyed coffee, fruit, and more *pan de bono,* and then our principals escorted us around the campus. The middle school wing, where I would be spending most of my time, was to the left of the main lounge and past the mail boxes. We passed out of the building onto a covered walkway which led to the different classrooms on the right.

"And here, Patricia - see, I remembered not to say Pot-- is your classroom," said Terry. As he unlocked the door, I saw my room for the first time. It was a small space with brick walls and one blackboard and one bulletin board. The eraser was no more than a wooden block with a piece of felt glued to one side. On the desk was one piece of chalk. I wrote "Pythagorean Theorem" on the board and then erased it just to see how, and if, the eraser worked; it worked just fine. A tiny desk for me (one drawer), one small storage cabinet and, about eighteen student desks completed the furnishings. The room would have been cozy had there been a fireplace, but that day it was just cold, and I wondered if it would be warmer when students were present.

After looking at other classrooms, the library, and the teacher's lounge, we all met back in the reception area to hear some last-minute instructions for Wednesday, the first day for all teachers to report for work. In department meetings and in-service workshops, we would receive teacher's editions, forms, calendars, materials and supplies. We were all anxious to meet the students in a week.

Excited about moving into our apartments the next day, we returned to the hotel to finish packing. In the ten days we had been in Bogotá we had accumulated a lot. Again, the school stepped in to help us move. Drivers and helpers were scheduled to arrive Thursday morning to help each group get settled before leaving us on our own.

With apartments chosen and our first visit to the school behind us, we were ready for a night out and decided to venture from the hotel dining room for our last night together. Only Doug and Martha and their three, tired children decided to eat in. Finding a pizza parlor close by, we had our first Colombian pizza. The restaurant was small and dimly lit and cozy. The few customers all seemed to be Colombian. Polite and somewhat formal, the waiter welcomed us and led us toward a table close to a roaring fireplace in the middle of the room. We sat as close to it as we could in an attempt to ward off the chill. The rain had started again that afternoon, and the warmth from the fire was soothing and comforting. I could smell the wet wool of my red ruana. For pizza toppings we ordered mushrooms and pepperoni. While waiting for dinner, we drank beer, smoked, and talked about everything that had happened during the last ten days. Most of us felt that, if we had to evacuate the next day, we had learned more about Colombian culture than we had ever dreamed possible. Would our learning curve continue this way? Would actually going to work change things? For better? Worse? Especially since we'd be, more or less, on our own. We still were not settled, but I think everybody felt more comfortable than they did that day we landed at El Dorado airport. We were adjusting and assimilating.

When the pizzas finally arrived, they were almost cool, not at all what you'd expect if they'd just come out of the oven. A nearby patron explained that at high altitudes food cools off quickly. So, with that bit of information we devoured our cool pizzas and noted the taste of a creamy, unrecognized cheese.

"Patricia," said Jerry, wiping tomato sauce from his chin, "Matt and I were wondering if you and Ellen could use some help tomorrow. It won't take us long to move our things."

"Of course. Thanks, Jerry," I replied, "I'm sure we could use the help, and company, too."

Soon, we wiped clean the pizza plates, emptied the beer glasses, and clapped our hands for the check. Clapping one's hands for the check was a new custom for us, and I couldn't imagine doing that if I were dining alone. It seemed a strange way to end a meal in a restaurant, but that's the way Colombians did it and I was determined to do what was expected. Pesos were beginning to seem like real money, too, as we counted our change to pay the bill.

When we returned to the hotel, we were in a festive mood that back home would have lead us to a club for late – night dancing and partying. But, taking a taxi at 10 p.m. in Bogotá might have been risky. Besides, that night, we were focused on moving out the next day, and no one wanted a hangover to sidetrack moving day.

Moving In

Storms rumbled through the mountains during the night, but by morning the plateau was sparkling and clear. Our drivers arrived at the hotel right on Colombian time, which, in this case, was only about forty minutes late. I hugged Jerry and Barb, said goodbye to everybody, and we all wished each other good luck as we packed our gear into the cars and headed off in different directions. By tomorrow, after sleeping one night in our apartments, we would go to work for the first full day for teachers.

Ellen and I had settled on an adequate, but not fancy, three-bedroom, third floor walkup with no view other than our neighbors' laundry areas and the back of an adjacent building. The apartment had two full baths, a spacious living/dining area, a tiny kitchen with gas stove and small refrigerator, and maid's quarters. The maid, arranged by the school, would arrive in a few days. At the entrance to the building there was a *portero* (guard) to let us in and out of the front door, and he and his family lived on the ground floor in a small apartment near where the residents parked their cars. Not us, of course: we didn't have cars. Even in this middle-class neighborhood, I was surprised that all the apartment buildings had porteros.

The main drawing card for the apartment was the location which was within two blocks of a large grocery store, several small shops and restaurants. The local bus line was close by and the school bus would pick us up one block from the apartment. Nearby was the only Sears store in Bogotá. In addition to selling appliances, it also had a buffet lunch counter. This was the Sears from which an American executive for that company was kidnapped a few weeks earlier. His two teenage children attended our school. Fortunately, he was released three months later, unharmed. National University was close by, and there were often demonstrations on campus, which required us to vary our route. Overall, it was considered a safe area, but no place was considered safe enough to let your guard down, ever.

Within an hour after Ellen and I arrived at the apartment, the movers from school showed up with our furniture. We each received a single bed, dresser, chest and lamp for our bedrooms and a large dining table, six chairs, a sofa, two easy chairs, a coffee table, and one end table for the living/dining area. The whole decorating situation suddenly became a non-issue. Since all of the import teachers had the same furnishings, there would be no need to concern ourselves with quality and style. Other than trinkets, we all had the same things in our apartments. What the school gave us was more than adequate, and whatever personal identity I had formerly linked to my surroundings would have to find some other place. It was going to be liberating.

With no air freight yet, we couldn't put sheets on the beds or set up the kitchen, but we did have enough dishes to survive a few days and were very grateful that our utilities were up and running, especially hot water for showers. We knew the telephone could take a few weeks, *palanca* or not, but it just didn't matter. We finally had a home! Dirty clothes were beginning to pile up, so we put the larger items on the bed and used our ruanas at night to stay warm and wore sweaters, socks, pantyhose, and anything else we could find to ward off the chill. The apartment had no central heat or air conditioning, but we really didn't need either. Some houses had fireplaces, which would have been welcome, but mostly, Colombians just dressed for the conditions and, depending on the need, either opened or closed the windows.

Soon after the movers left, Jerry and Matt showed up, and we all made a quick run to the grocery store before settling in. Ellen and I needed a coffee maker and decided on a device called a *calcetin,* which we had seen at the hotel. A sock hangs on a metal frame and is removed and washed after each use. Coffee grounds are placed in the bottom of the sock and then boiling water is poured on top. Colombian coffee that drips into the cup is rich, fragrant and addictive. Clean-up was going to be messy, but we were willing to deal with the inconvenience while we waited for our household boxes to arrive. At the grocery store we also bought bread, sandwich meat, cheese, mayonnaise, mustard, fruit, and juice in cartons, all things we could have bought in the States. With the few things we had picked up earlier we felt we would have enough to get us through breakfast and lunch until the weekend when we could make a more substantial purchase. For dinner we'd have to shop again or eat out. With no car, we filled our backpacks at the grocery store. Without Jerry and Matt, Ellen and I probably couldn't have carried everything, and I made a mental note to plan carefully when I went alone. Grocery shopping wasn't the first time I had missed my car.

We picked up some empanadas, little meat-filled pies, from a corner kiosko and had a quick meal at home. With nothing much to do for the rest of the evening, Jerry and Matt left, and I washed out a few clothes. We had detergent but couldn't figure out how to set up the maid's washroom so we used the bathroom sinks and draped our lingerie around the shower stall. When the maid arrived soon, laundry was going to be one of her biggest responsibilities, one that we would gladly relinquish. With no washing machine or dryer, I was really curious about how she would wash sheets, towels, and clothes, dry them, and then do the ironing. And all in such a small space.

But now, the night before the first work day, I was feeling a little disconnected and unsettled. When Ellen and I went to our own rooms, I rummaged through my few belongings. We had no TV, or, of course, telephone, my radio was with my air freight; there were no papers to grade yet. I had finished the paperback books I carried with me from the States and hadn't picked up anything new to read. Through my window I could hear city noises in the dark and wondered what some of them were. The only things I had to occupy myself were paper and pen so I started writing letters to family and friends and continued doing so for my entire year. Writing home was how I coped with the estrangement from all familiar things, a simple panacea when loneliness crept in.

When the alarm clock blared at 5:15 a.m., I jumped out of bed in a heartbeat. A morning person to the core, I practically ran to the kitchen, put on the water to boil for the coffee, and headed to the bathroom for a quick shower. Ellen and I had agreed to use our own clocks to wake up so I didn't notice that she was still in bed until I finished in the bathroom and went back to the kitchen for breakfast. My food was stored in the refrigerator on the right and hers on the left. My carefully planned meal that morning was to be a box of pineapple juice, with bread and coffee. When I reached in for the juice, it wasn't there! There was no juice anywhere! Then I decided to check on Ellen and found her still asleep with two empty juice boxes on her nightstand.

"ELLEN, it's almost six o'clock! We have to meet the bus at 6:30 today! Get up!" I stared in disbelief as she moaned and rolled over. She opened her eyes, but made no effort to get up. Concerned that she might be sick, I held off mentioning anything about the juice. "Are you okay? Is something wrong."

Finally, she mumbled that she had not been able to sleep last night... "I'll get up. It's okay."

I backed out of the room and listened for some sign that she meant it, and when I finally heard water running, I went back to kitchen, ate my bread, and poured a cup of coffee.

We reached the bus stop on time, and later on that afternoon I asked her about the juice. She admitted to having had a panic attack the night before and, yes, she drank all the juice and ate all the sandwich meat. She offered no apologies, just a sadness that had crept in. I didn't have the heart to be angry because I could sense things were not right with her.

A Final Fling

I had every reason in the world to be excited about the first day back at school. Not only would I have the opportunity to work at a job I loved, but I'd also be meeting dozens of new faculty members in a totally new environment. I expected my life to be enriched. Throughout that first day of introductions, food, and academic discussions, I felt an air of anticipation unequaled by any I had experienced in the workplace. I hoped it would continue. The Principal, Terry, invited all Middle School teachers to a party Friday night. All faculty members were invited to a barbecue on Saturday night and to Phyllis' finca Sunday before the students arrived on Monday. Everybody seemed happy as we piled up on the buses that afternoon and headed back home. Our maid would come by the apartment Friday afternoon to meet Ellen and me so we had a lot to look forward to.

I barely saw Ellen that first day at work, but when we arrived back at the apartment, she was obviously distressed. After I mentioned her refrigerator-raiding episode the night before, she just withdrew. Hoping hers was a temporary adjustment problem, I tried to reassure her and offer support, but she was unresponsive and uncommunicative. She went to her room early and stayed there. At a loss, I busied myself with new textbooks.

The next day at school was full of meetings to prepare for our students who would arrive next week. Around 11:00 a.m. several of us heard that our airfreight had arrived, and the bus from school would take us to Customs to pick up the boxes. We'd have to unpack everything while authorities watched before they released anything. Having learned to hold our comments in dealing with the Government, we watched with frustration as guards ripped open box tops and tossed around our household goods. When, finally, they were satisfied we weren't bringing in drugs or contraband, we were told to come back tomorrow and pick it all up. Mañana! That seemed to be the philosophy of life here. We were learning that if you didn't have a lot of patience, you soon developed it as a means of coping. I supposed one more night without sheets wouldn't matter, so, mañana, we'd head down there again.

Before leaving school on Friday, the director called a security meeting because there had been more than the usual anti-American rumblings in the city. The school and the American Embassy were always in touch, and we heard once more of the need for watchfulness.

Ellen and I made a quick trip to Customs, picked up our boxes with no delays and headed home. Receiving our personal belongings felt like Christmas! My sheets and pillowcases still had a freshly laundered scent, the old electric coffeepot looked new, and the extra clothes and personal items were just as welcome as if they had been gifts. I couldn't wait to get my space organized.

The new maid, Angela, stopped by that afternoon. She spoke no English but seemed to enjoy my attempts to speak in Spanish. Ellen was, again, remote and disengaged, didn't have any opinions about the arrangements, and wasn't willing to try any Spanish. We were going to experiment with a Monday, Wednesday, and Friday schedule when Angela would clean, wash and iron clothes, and cook for our night meal. Monday would be wash day so we went over what she would need and what we would need to prepare.

Just before time to leave for the party at Terry's house, Barb, another Middle School teacher, arrived. Barb and I were looking forward to a fun evening, but worried about Ellen staying home. Ellen taught High School and was therefore not going to Terry's but had been invited out by some other teachers. She gave no reason for not going.

Since transportation was always a challenge, especially at night, we took a taxi to Terry's house after being told that someone from school would take us home. Knowing we wouldn't have to be on the streets late at night meant we could relax and enjoy the party. I really missed my car, but, to be honest, I would have been terrified to drive anywhere in Bogotá, even in the daytime, and couldn't imagine driving at night there.

The Bogotanos I'd met at school were charming, friendly people, a little reserved, perhaps, and proud of their cultural heritage; they considered Bogotá to be the Athens of South America. So, I was expecting a rather formal, receiving line at the party that wouldn't last long. What a surprise! When Barb and I arrived at 9:45, nearly fifty people were already there. It was just not possible to be somewhere at a certain time when dependent on public transportation, so, of course we were apologetic for being late. How unnecessary. Time seemed to have a different meaning in Colombia; punctuality was not a big issue. Back home, I couldn't imagine showing up for a reception forty-five minutes late at Mr. Mayo's house (or my dad's).

Terry's house was large and warm, thanks to two fireplaces whose roaring flames were a peculiar shade of gold, and typical of the local homes I had visited: muted colors, leather furniture, local artifacts displayed on the walls, and no view at all of the kitchen. I had begun to wonder if the electric companies rationed power or if the dimness was due to other factors. Even in the daytime, the interiors were dark because the few windows tended to be small and high on the walls. Were they another concession to the need for tight security? At any rate, Terry and his Colombian wife were gracious and generous hosts. A butler served as the bartender, and two maids passed trays of hors d'oeuvres throughout the evening. Probably more help worked in the kitchen. The drinks served were scotch, daiquiris, and aguardiente. Aguardiente is a Colombian drink distilled from the sugar cane that tastes like rubbing alcohol and licorice. It is VERY potent and often mixed with fruit drinks or Coca-Cola, which reminded me of a college favorite. I had lost a taste for PJ long ago and didn't enjoy the aguardiente, so I stuck with the daiquiris.

In the background was wistful, rhythmic Colombian music. Soft and soulful but not without joy, it was perfect music for this type of gathering, which the Americans thought would be over by 11:00 p.m. Not a chance! At precisely 11:00 we were ushered into a room that had been cleared for dancing, and that's when the evening really came to life. We learned some basic moves for native Colombian dances and held candles while trying the "Cumbia," an erotic dance with African roots. The man follows the woman who carries candles high in the air while she undulates voluptuously, turning constantly on the same spot. She brings the flames closer to his face each time she turns, and at a certain point, he gyrates in the opposite direction with his head thrown back, and then she dances toward him. We did our best to swirl and gyrate and toss our hair while being mindful of the candles. Fortunately, we survived the Cumbia without doing any damage to each other or the house.

After our stabs at other Colombian folk dances, we also did the good old U.S. "bump," which the Colombians seemed to enjoy more than we did. They pronounced it "boomp" and did it very well. Didn't hear a bit of beach music. The party went on until 3:00 a.m. when nearly everyone collapsed from exhaustion. At that time drivers hired just for the purpose gave us rides home. We had now been properly welcomed by a typical Colombian party.

The Students Arrive

By the time Sunday afternoon rolled around, we were exhausted and in need of the routine provided by getting up each morning and going to work. I knew that the professional responsibility would be a calming factor in my hectic existence at that moment, and I was ready for whatever the job might bring.

The first week with my students was typically demanding and revealing. The first thing I noticed about my new students was their size – they were smaller than their U.S. counterparts, and all were well-dressed and well-mannered. The school had chosen through the years not to require students to wear uniforms, but their self-imposed uniform seemed to be jeans, t-shirts, sneakers and some kind of jacket or ruana. One curly-haired boy from Switzerland wore lederhosen every day, and, like girls everywhere at that age, the young women experimented a lot with makeup. But all students were clean and neat, and their appearance was never an issue.

These kids were focused on school work and had goals. They wanted to learn and were eager for everything I had to offer. English was the second language for most, and we all shared many opportunities for them, and me, too, to refine our language skills. When a student told me one time he couldn't "make" his homework, I was startled for a moment and then realized the Spanish verb *"hacer"* means "to make" or "do." So, in some respects, they were just like teenagers everywhere, when they were not "doing" their homework or not "making" it. That rarely happened, but it was a moment of linguistic clarity for that young man and me.

The students were friendly and engaging, too, with a surprising amount of sophistication and social skills. They frequently asked about me and how I was getting along in Bogotá and what did I think of former President Nixon leaving office and did I like the Rolling Stones. These were twelve- and thirteen-year-olds. If there was anything amiss, even ever so slightly, it was that a number of them seemed lonely and in need of another adult in their lives who cared about them. As their teacher, I was glad and honored that they came to me for that support. Most of the families had live-in domestic help, and I could only guess which parents left the child-rearing responsibility almost exclusively to the maids.

The parents I met in the coming months were actively involved with school activities and were cooperative and supportive. These parents, who were grooming their children for the top universities all over the world, spared no gesture in providing a creative and productive environment, including positive relations with the teachers. I was not accustomed to receiving gifts from parents on a regular basis, but it was not unusual for a student to bring me a nice bottle of wine from his parents, or a hand-painted flower vase or even the offer of a weekend at their finca with my friends. I told myself such generosity was just a cultural thing and not to get used to it. But they were generous, and that generosity certainly affected my own demeanor and maybe caused me to have a little more patience at times and work a little harder. Whenever I had to contact parents regarding their child's performance, they always listened to me attentively and promptly heeded any suggestions.

The school, the students, the parents, the faculty and support personnel became my stabilizing force in Colombia and were a part of my life as much as my friends and family back home. When professional challenges came, I felt valued and knew I had made the right decision in accepting this job.

Roommates And Becoming Southern

In the 1960s, efforts by the Colombian military to eradicate pockets of guerilla resistance in rural areas were often thwarted by groups such as the Revolutionary Armed Forces of Colombia (FARC). The 1970s had ushered in a growing disorder in the urban areas of Colombia, as well, and Bogotá, being the capital, was often targeted. The military, working with the police, had responsibility for breaking up illegal strikes and student demonstrations, which frequently resulted in closing the Universities. By mid-decade, assassinations, kidnappings, bombings, and other acts of urban terrorism posed a serious threat to domestic order. In September 1975, not long after our arrival, the Army's Inspector General was assassinated, and the concerns about our safety increased. The city was in a constant state of siege, and, for us, that meant frequently staying home from work and seeing more policemen on the streets, who carried more and bigger firearm. We received phone calls late at night telling us school was canceled the next day because of political unrest, as it always was on election days. The women in our group were told not to leave our apartments unless there was an emergency, and so we stayed in and rested or did school work. On election days I wondered about the Colombian women not voting and was told later that private drivers or bodyguards took upper-class women to the polls, but many husbands did not allow women out of their houses because of the danger. For the first time I really thought about the privilege of voting as something other than a God-given right, and certainly for the first time I was living in a country where being able to cast one's vote was not taken for granted.

On those days when school was canceled, friends would often gather in our apartment as Ellen and I were in a central location. In spite of the suggestions that we stay inside, there was a need to be with colleagues, and none of our group had problems getting to our barrio. We would eat, talk, and try to find out what was going on by listening to the radio and waiting for phone calls. On one such afternoon the talk turned to teachers who were hired by CNG and what some of the unstated qualifications were.

"I've heard they don't hire teachers from the South because the parents don't want their children picking up Southern accents," Matt said. "I mean, do you know any teachers here from the South?" forgetting there were several import teachers from the South.

"Yeah, can you imagine a teacher saying things like 'I ain't got no problem with y'all writin' on both sides of the paper'?" said Jerry. As if all Southerners said things like that.

There were some cheap laughs all around and, as my antennae went up, I bristled when I considered that many people felt that way about Southerners.

"Whoa, guys, I'm from North Carolina, and that's in the South. Bruce and Movelle are from Tennessee. Do you think we sound like that? What in the hell are you talking about?" I blurted out, becoming more defensive with each passing moment.

"Oh, you don't have that accent. It's the one from, you know, oh, I don't know, wherever it is they talk like that." Jerry struggled to pull his foot out of his mouth and seemed sincerely contrite.

It was the first time I had ever encountered personal discrimination based on my Southern roots and I was shocked. I had grown up in an educated family; both of my parents and two sisters had graduate degrees, as did most of my aunts and uncles and cousins. My grandparents had attended college, and my great-grandfather was a physician who performed the first successful appendectomy in North Carolina. The more I steamed, the more I thought about the accomplishments of those I loved and wondered if I would always be defending them as I defended myself, just because we were Southern. Discrimination was alive and well in the United States and was justifiably fueling the Civil Rights movement, but never had I personally felt on the receiving end of such ignorance. Prejudice was something we were expecting to encounter from Colombians against Americans or Americans against Colombians, but non-Southerners against Southerners? I was furious and definitely took it all personally. From that day on I had a new perspective on my Southern heritage and openly challenged anyone who directed their misconceptions to me.

Efforts were made to correct the faux pas, but I was insulted for a long time. Eventually I got over it and I never heard another reference to a Southern accent. I'd like to think that some of my colleagues learned a little something about tolerance after that exchange.

A month after Ellen and I moved into the apartment, Ellen was waiting for an aunt to come to Bogotá and escort her back to the States. Whatever caused her to decide to leave I'll never know, but I could only wish her well. The school, of course, helped with her plans and assisted in the complicated transition out of the country. Her departure happened so fast that I didn't even know when she left. One day when I came home from work, her personal belongings were gone. A school administrator had told me that day she would be leaving, and I was disturbed and surprised to see her disappear so fast. Ellen, with her halo of blond curls, and dreams and aspirations like the rest of us, chose to opt out.

Almost immediately my principal, Terry, told me about another teacher who was living alone with her adopted daughter and was looking for someone to share expenses. Would I be interested in such an arrangement? Dot Onufer was in her second year at CNG. She had spent a year at Jorge Washington School in Cartagena and came to Bogotá when she decided to adopt a child. I hadn't considered living with someone with children but was not opposed at all to the idea. My own nieces and nephews were so dear to me that I couldn't imagine children being a problem. Besides, I had an apartment large enough to accommodate all three of us, plus the live-in maid we'd need.

Soon, Dot invited Jerry and me for dinner. She was living in a small, one-bedroom apartment without maid's quarters and was feeling understandably cramped. In spite of her tiny kitchen, she prepared a delicious meal, including *arroz con coco,* rice with coconut, a popular coastal dish she had learned to prepare when she lived in Cartagena. We seemed to get along well and decided that moving in together would suit both of us if my apartment suited her needs. When we left, Jerry and I both felt she would make a great roommate. She was very focused on her child, Lucía, and her job, and there was little chance she would be leaving Bogotá soon. Plus, after two years in Colombia, her Spanish was better than mine.

Soon Dot and little Luci moved in. Angela found a position with another CNG family, and the new maid, Selena, moved in with her baby. So there we were: Selena and her baby, Dot and her new daughter, and me.

It was easy to adjust to the new living arrangements. Little Luci didn't cry at night, Selena's baby rarely made a peep, and dinner was always ready. Our clothes were washed and ironed, the apartment was cleaned, and I had few domestic responsibilities. Occasionally, there would be no hot water, or no water at all, or no gas or electricity. If we needed help, we called the school and almost immediately, our problems were solved. So, Dot and I moved on and continued exploring the city and culture.

Roommate Dot Onufer, her daughter Lucía,
and Patricia, Bogotá, 1975.

One night, after a long, tiring day, I drifted off to sleep without reading anything. I was so tired I don't remember my head hitting my pillow.

Jerry and Matt were dancing. I had never noticed that their bodies were so lean and taut. They were wearing tight, black, high-waisted, matador pants with suspenders. Their shirts were white with a black design, (hearts, maybe?), with starched, buttoned-down collars and long sleeves, with red ties that draped gracefully almost to their waists. The music was a strange combination of tango and salsa with more than a touch of southern blues. The intensity on their faces seemed perfunctory and, while their bodies moved skillfully in synch, as if they had been dancing together for years, there was no tenderness or pleasure. They were just dancing, and I was mesmerized. I wanted to dance.

Ellen was in the kitchen, scraping the layers of fat off a picnic ham.

It was too late to be driving home alone at night, but I was sleepy. My eyes kept closing, and I struggled to stay awake. When my car stalled at a stoplight, I could barely turn the ignition, and I waited for the car behind me to blow its horn. It never did, but finally pulled out and slowly passed me. Did anyone notice that I might need help? I was giving in to sleep, sweet sleep, and then I was trying to wake up again. My body slumped over once more, and all I wanted was unconsciousness. Two shadowy figures circled the car, and I was suddenly frightened out of my slumber. I bolted upright and....

With my heart pounding, gasping for breath and drenched in sweat, I woke up. A dream! A nightmare? Angry and confused, I tossed my comforter off the bed and willed my heart rate slowly back to normal. I took some deep breaths and waited to calm down. When I felt safe getting up, I went to the kitchen for a glass of water and wondered where my anxiety had come from. Vivid dreams were usual for me, and I gained little by overanalyzing. As long as a dream didn't disrupt my sleep too much, I didn't really mind. Maybe it had something to do with a blind date I had agreed to for the following week.

The Red Ruana And First Date

September and October were filled with excursions around the city: trips to the magnificent Gold Museum and the house of the great Liberator, Simón Bolívar, a night at the Ballet Folklórico and shopping excursions where we searched for local arts and crafts, called *típicos*. Trips always meant meals with local specialties.

One excursion, in particular, provided a reality check on the safety issue that lurked in the background relentlessly. It reminded me that threats to our own personal safety were real and our complacency should not be allowed to interfere with our better judgment.

Barb and I had heard about a government-owned co-op in *el centro* that sold the best and most original handicrafts in Bogotá: weavings, artwork, Christmas decorations, sweaters, ruanas and many other items from all over the country. Even though we had been told to avoid that area, we felt confident enough to hail a taxi one Saturday morning and go straight to the front door of the store. We didn't plan to walk around the area.

Getting there was easy. Our Spanish had improved, and we were familiar enough with the city by then that we could give directions to a driver and know if he was heading to the right *barrio*. He took us exactly where we wanted to go, and, as we stepped out of the taxi, I was immediately assaulted by the sounds, the smells and hordes of people. I could hear the cars and buses roaring through the streets blasting their horns, sounding as if they were on loudspeakers. I could smell exhaust fumes and empanadas and a sweet soap many of the people used. Everyone seemed to be one beat away from a jog as they headed to their destinations and shoved and pushed up against each other on the street. Some men wore suits and carried briefcases; (most of the people *were* men), and others were dressed casually. Many wore *ruanas* even though the sun was intense that day with no suggestion of rain. The cold Andean wind, however, which never let up, seemed to propel people along. Everybody was on the move; everybody, that is, except the beggars and children who ambled slowly among the crowd, hands outstretched, pleading.

Barb and I dodged the activity and entered the store without incident. Looking around, we realized quickly that this was exactly the place we had been looking for. For a couple of hours we looked, touched the fabrics, tried on sweaters and discussed the artwork we could hang on the walls of our apartments. We then marveled at the skill and talent of the people who had made these beautiful items.

We made our purchases and, wearing full backpacks and carrying a few shopping bags, headed back outside with plans to quickly hail a taxi and return home.

What we didn't anticipate was that it was lunch time, and finding a taxi would be a waiting game. The number of people on the street had increased, and every time we stepped off the curb to hail a driver, someone else would step up and jump in the car before we could make a move. We did a lot of swearing that day and didn't care at all if anybody heard because we knew they wouldn't understand. After watching the traffic patterns, we finally decided to cross the street for a better chance of getting a ride. Our bags were heavy, and we were gradually becoming aware of how we looked: two white females, Barb, a tall striking pale brunette in a navy ruana and me, a tall blond in a red ruana, both carrying shopping bags. Obviously not local people. We weren't wearing jewelry or miniskirts, but our hair was long and flying, and we must have been targeted the minute we stepped out of the store.

Before long a taxi stopped, and we stepped into the cab with great relief. The atmosphere was getting uncomfortable, and we were anxious to get out of *el centro*. We told the driver the address. I was seated behind him and Barb was to my right. I had just relaxed my arms around my bags when the driver looked at something behind us and then to the side. With no warning, the car door suddenly opened on my side, and a man pushed me over and grabbed my bags. His foul smell was sickening. Our eyes met for a moment but there was nothing there. Barb screamed; I tightened my grasp on the bags, and the driver turned around and shoved the guy out of the car. The would-be thief was too disoriented to struggle and fell on the pavement as the driver slammed my door, and we sped off. I doubt if anybody on the street even blinked an eye while this was happening.

On the way back to the apartment Barb and I thanked the driver as we tried to calm ourselves down and realized we had just had a close call. A thief wouldn't hesitate to hurt us if he wanted something, and we vowed to be even more conscious of our appearance. I never wore the red ruana anywhere close to *el centro* again and eventually bought another one in a dark color. My hair stayed blond, but I started pulling it back in a ponytail or covered by a hat or scarf in public.

The incident unsettled me for a long time and was compounded by a sad event which happened a few days later.

A vivid impression in the city was the sight of young boys, street kids, flying down the hills on rickety, homemade contraptions like skateboards, only slightly longer and wider. They carry newspapers, cardboard boxes, and make a living selling it by weight. It's fascinating and terrifying to watch them weave in and out of traffic. They have the same looks on their faces as kids in amusement parks who crave the thrill of roller coasters. They are called, affectionately, *gamines.*

One morning on the way to school, our bus was turning off the plateau on the northern side of the city and beginning the ascent into the hills when the bus slowed down and I noticed extra traffic. People on the street were pointing just ahead where a hairpin curve and steep hill met. While waiting for the road to clear, our driver was talking to somebody outside the bus. Word quickly reached us that a city bus had hit and killed one of the *gamines,* and the area was now being cleaned up. After a short while our bus was allowed to pass and right there, on the street, was the blood-stained pavement where the boy had been hit. The smear on the street was still red. As we chugged up the hill and I took a deep breath, I noticed the students remained quiet. I guessed we were all trying to absorb the shock of what we had just witnessed. The young people on the bus obviously had had more experience than we, the import teachers, had in dealing with this kind of tragedy so there was nothing really for us to say to them. Again, as I watched them accept another of those realities involving the poor and underprivileged people in Bogotá, I felt frustrated and baffled. Why weren't these young boys on skateboards in school? And where were the young girls? Was anybody overseeing their welfare? How long did their zest and exuberance last, and to what end? The rest of the day was uneventful and somber, and I felt as if I were drifting alone through a fog. When I finally arrived home that afternoon, I felt profoundly violated. Yes, it was a sad day, and I was emotionally drained.

Almost immediately after these two events a teacher approached me at school, whom I had not yet met, Maria Isabel Rojas. Of French and Colombian heritage, she was married to a Colombian and had taught at CNG since moving to Bogotá a few years earlier. She asked if I would be interested in meeting a friend of theirs, Paul, a North American, who had lived several years in Colombia. Since his father's death several years earlier, Paul had managed the family construction business in Latin America. Maria Isabel vouched for Paul, and I felt it was safe enough to meet him. I eagerly embraced the prospect of finding somebody to go out with, especially after recent events. After a phone call a few days later, we made plans for dinner on the weekend. It was a great boost to my spirits, and I started thinking immediately about what I would wear. By Saturday, I was looking forward to dinner out with a new man.

Time in Colombia was always nebulous. Prompt to a fault, perhaps, I took it for granted that everybody else, if they had good intentions, was on time. Gradually, however, I soon accepted the impossibility of knowing that you could be somewhere at a certain time in a city. When I was growing up in the small town of Whiteville, in North Carolina, if a boy said he would be there at 7:30, he was there. Throughout college and then when I moved to New Bern, people still seemed to get places on time. So, when Paul was forty-five minutes late for our first date, I was sure I had been stood up and was thoroughly miffed. How could Maria Isabel set me up with somebody like this? I was getting ready to change clothes when the *portero* called from downstairs saying Paul had arrived. Begrudgingly, I gave permission for him to come up and thought about how to handle the situation appropriately.

I took my time unlocking the three locks on the door and when I opened it, what I saw didn't impress me at all: a rather short, fair, middle-aged man with close-cropped hair, and not even an attempt at a smile.

"Paul? Come in. I'll get my things."

"Thank you. Sorry I'm late, but the traffic was blocked at the entrance to the barrio because of an accident. Typical for a Saturday night."

"It's OK," I offered, "I'll be right back." (So much for "handling" the situation).

Within minutes we were down the stairs, out of the building and into his car. The *portero* locked the entrance gate behind us.

Paul plowed into the traffic. Navigating the streets of Bogotá on a Saturday night, he had no time for chit chat. Communication would have to wait, so I looked out the window and watched the city unfold, hoping this man was not as surly as he appeared. "Oh, well," I thought, "this is what dating is all about." I tried to adjust my expectations. It wasn't until we came within a block of the restaurant that Paul started talking.

"A few weeks ago, a man who was leaving this restaurant with his wife was gunned down here on the sidewalk."

"What? Who did it? Why? Was it robbery?"

"No. It wasn't robbery. Probably terrorist activity related to the drug traffic. That's the way they make their point," Paul said, as he slipped into the valet parking spot. "Who were 'they'," I thought.

As we approached the restaurant door, my heart was pounding, and I glanced at the sidewalk looking for blood stains, which weren't there. Paul seemed very calm, and I came to find out that evening that it was not unusual for drive-by murders to happen at the most respectable places. The best restaurants, hotels, office buildings, even private homes had all seen horrific crimes related to the drug war. That night, however, as we sat at a small table in a romantic alcove, I took a deep breath, knowing that I was flushed, and looked at the menu, trying to concentrate on the evening ahead and salvage something of this anticipated night out.

Casa Vieja, an elegant, understated restaurant that specialized in Colombian dishes, apparently catered to a genteel, sophisticated clientele, including upper crust *narcotraficantes.* As Paul and I gradually found our own rhythm, he told me even more about the life style of the drug traffickers: their children went to the best private schools (I had already heard rumors that some of these children were at CNG), the women were elegant and well-educated. They had lavish homes, exotic vacations and ever-present security to protect them. ("From whom," I thought, "each other?") He also talked about the not uncommon murders often carried out by thugs in broad daylight.

Paul ordered a Chilean wine and described the entrees. He suggested a local specialty, *ajiaco,* a rich, chicken soup served with many condiments. As we sipped the wine and enjoyed a crisp, green salad and a fresh, warm loaf of bread, he started talking about his work in Costa Rica. His company was presently bulldozing through the jungle there to build new roads, and he was traveling between Bogotá and the sites. He predicted that most American concerns in Latin America would probably end operations within five years because of the economy and unstable political conditions here. I just listened while he talked, and talked, about his business. All I could offer to the conversation was the little I knew about the two-party political system that alternated Conservative and Liberal presidents. In 1974 the system was actually phased out, but the Constitution required that the losing political party be given adequate participation. Many thought this led to an increase in corruption, and Paul agreed. Finally, the *ajiaco* arrived and I was grateful for an opportunity to concentrate on eating.

It was a big bowl of soup, steaming and fragrant, with chunks of chicken, potatoes and leaves of cilantro floating in a clear, golden, peppery broth. Separate bowls of condiments appeared simultaneously, intended to be added to the soup before eating: capers, avocados, corn slices about one-inch thick, more cilantro, all to be topped off with a dollop of fresh cream.

I slowly prepared my soup, examining the ingredients I ladled into my bowl. I watched Paul to see how he handled the corn. The corn I had eaten in the past was creamed, sliced from the cob or either on the cob seasoned with butter, salt and pepper. Dealing with these disks was a new experience for me.

My first tentative sip of broth burst with sinus-clearing piquancy. Once all the ingredients were blended and a bit of avocado mixed with the capers, I was a convert and knew this soup would become my favorite Colombian dish. It was heavenly. The corn was still to come so, when Paul scooped up a piece with his spoon and tossed the whole thing in his mouth, I watched closely, wondering if he would swallow it as a sort of male ritual like eating the worm at the bottom of a tequila bottle. Just as quickly, he put his spoon down, took the corn out of his mouth with his fingers and chewed the kernels until the core was clean and then put the remains on the side of his plate. I had no choice but to try so, I followed his lead; picked up the corn with my spoon and placed it on my tongue. I had to suck the juices from the corn before opening my mouth again, and then another burst of mouth-watering intensity hit my palate. I reached in with my fingers, picked up the corn, and slowly chewed my way around the core. By the time I was finished, my chin was dripping, and I was reaching for my napkin. Paul didn't seem to notice any of this, thankfully, and we continued with our meal, and I had learned how to eat sliced corn.

At almost 11 p.m., when we finished our last cups of *tinto,* Paul suggested we stop by an outdoor café where he often met friends. We could have dessert, an after-dinner drink and enjoy sitting outside. Fresh air sounded good after the dark, confining restaurant.

Oma's was a relatively new spot with an outdoor seating area on a major thoroughfare in the northern part of the city. Popular with the locals and expats, it attracted an artsy, bohemian, and upscale crowd, if not all at the same time. Everything about the barrio seemed new and modern: the buildings, store fronts and merchandise in the windows, even the roads. I was curious to know the funding for this development, but never had a chance, that night, to ask. I had my ideas, though.

When we walked in, people immediately greeted Paul, and we joined eight people sitting outside on the patio. The cool air and brisk wind created an oasis, and, even at midnight, I felt rejuvenated. The people were friendly and welcoming, and I couldn't help notice that some of the men were without dates/companions/wives. After crème-de-menthe crepes and coffee, Paul finished his night with cognac. Conversation was comfortable, and I felt very content among these people and hoped I'd spend time with them again. When we finally left, I had to admit that the date with Paul hadn't been the disaster I had feared. I had been treated to a wonderful meal, met new people, and discovered a new part of the city.

My feelings about Paul were less clear. He was certainly a good person to know in my current situation, but I wasn't sure there was a spark between us. Only time would tell, and I wondered how much physical attraction should matter anyway. He was leaving the next day for Costa Rica and asked if I would be interested in going to Melgar with him and a group of friends when he got back to Bogotá. Could I find a date for one of his friends? What he told me about the place sounded intriguing, so I said yes and mentally started packing summer clothes.

Demonstrations And Omar Shariff

Back at school, our first grading period was ending and instead of sending out report cards, parent conferences were scheduled over a two-day period. Teachers would meet with each set of parents fifteen minutes, so it was important to be well prepared with an in-depth analysis of each child's progress. It was a new way for me to report grades, and I spent a lot of time preparing. We were expected to speak English and be concise.

When the first set of parents arrived and their fifteen minutes flew by, I was relieved. I dealt with their questions well and helped develop a trusting relationship. The parents were warm, friendly, and sincerely interested in their child's development, so it was easy to talk to them. They were also knowledgeable about Math. Our next set of grades would be on paper, but this first contact with the parents was a highlight of my professional experience at CNG. The sense of community and respect that evolved from these face-to-face encounters definitely enhanced the learning experience – for students, teachers, and parents.

All conferences ended by 1 p.m. on the second day, and to celebrate, parents and the school provided lunch for the faculty and staff. After the administration acknowledged our contributions and talents, we ate a delicious, late lunch of ravioli, salad, bread, and a hearty red wine.

It was a time to relax, talk about upcoming plans and the news. We'd read about the second assassination attempt on President Ford, Patty Hearst and her abduction by the Symbionese Liberation Army. We knew that Franco, deposed dictator of Spain, was near death. The Russian Embassy in Bogotá was bombed, but no injuries were reported. The bombings, demonstrations and assassinations didn't elicit much response from the local teachers, at least in our presence, but we craved any and all news, especially from the States. When an international edition of TIME magazine was sometimes available, we passed it around gingerly whenever we could get our hands on a copy. It cost approximately $1 US. Someone at our table reported on an International Bridge Tournament in Bogotá at the Hilton Hotel where Omar Sharif would be competing. Since most of us knew him from the movie, *Dr. Zhivago*, and were impressed with his celebrity and heart-throb good looks, we made plans to find out more and maybe try to see him.

It was a great afternoon after parent conferences and our group of import teachers felt secure and happy. If we ever questioned our decision to make this commitment in a land so far from home, it wasn't on that day. That day we reveled in our perseverance and knew that we were reaping some of the rewards. Warmed by the wine and the satisfaction that comes from doing a job well, we settled into our niches and acknowledged our debt to CNG for making it all possible. They were taking good care of us.

A few days later, the school received calls from the American Embassy and authorities in Washington, D.C., ordering us to dismiss classes immediately. They expected demonstrations that afternoon in downtown Bogotá and possibly at the American Embassy as well. Evacuation plans went into effect immediately, and within thirty minutes all classrooms were empty and the entire fleet of buses was on the road. All we found out before leaving was that anti-American factions were protesting President Lopez' upcoming trip to the U.S., and we knew nothing about that. As we wound our way through an unfamiliar route to the students' homes, I looked outside for signs of unusual activity and saw nothing out of the ordinary. The students, old pros at this kind of disruption, sat in their seats and chatted quietly with their classmates, but I could sense an uneasiness and tension in the air. I wondered which ones had been affected personally by the constant political and social disturbances, as many of them surely had, and wondered even more about the resources they called on to deal with these events. They all reached home safely, and when Dot and I got off the bus and started walking the short distance to the apartment, we realized that we, too, were anxious and jittery. Everybody we saw looked suspicious, and we were almost running.

Comic relief came quickly when we opened the apartment door and saw Selena, standing at the ironing board, ironing our underwear. There were neat stacks of bras, panties, and nightgowns, things we never ironed back home, all arranged by the owner. The two babies were seated on a pallet on the floor, quietly gurgling and playing. Colombian country music was coming from the radio. There couldn't have been a more tranquil scene. We tried hard not to let Selena see our surprise because, of course, it was a luxurious treat to have our underwear ironed, and we appreciated it, but that day, at that time, it was just hysterical. Our worry about the demonstrations and the confusion and chaos of the day exploded in belly laughs I didn't know I had. As we laughed and cried at the same time, we told Selena we had heard a funny joke, hoping she wouldn't think we were laughing at her, because we weren't. We were just releasing tension, and the ironed underwear was a convenient catalyst.

When Jerry, Matt and Barb soon joined us, we spent the rest of the afternoon listening to the radio, trying to understand the reports. Matt had heard that crowds were gathering in *el centro* and that the military police were out in full force. It wasn't long before we received a call from Terry, the principal, wanting to know if we were OK and who was with us. In situations of potential violence, they kept close tabs on all of us. School was canceled for the following day, and Terry reminded us to be careful and stay close to the phone. We were in a holding mode – like receiving hurricane warnings in North Carolina and then waiting for the storm to arrive. And like the hurricanes, which could deliver a puff of wind or just as easily a catastrophic disaster, the threats of violence were disturbing and made us all anxious.

The riots never did materialize. A lot of unrest continued but we soon returned to school with heightened security and a little better understanding of life in Bogotá.

Our interests soon turned to more innocent pursuits when news of Omar Sharif was confirmed. Several of us made plans to stop by the Hilton on the day he was scheduled to arrive. The hotel would give us no information, so we decided to stop after school hoping to glimpse the movie star. It was my second trip to the Hilton; the first was for a hair trim, color and facial. The beauty parlor was a plush excursion, and many of us indulged occasionally, especially since the cost was a reasonable $20 US. On this day, however, we were looking forward to finding comfortable seats in the lobby where there seemed to be as many waiters as guests. Perhaps we didn't look like vagabonds, but, with our backpacks, ruanas and school clothes, no one could have mistaken us for international jet-set guests.

We found a spot with four club chairs, a huge plant, and an imposing column, which we hoped would make us inconspicuous. Our plan was to sit quietly and try to blend in while waiting for Mr. Sharif to pass. Immediately, a polite young waiter took our order, which, on Jerry's recommendation, was Brandy Alexanders for all. The milk sounded soothing so we ordered that and kept our eyes focused on the front door and elevators. When the drinks arrived, they tasted like chocolate milk. We sipped and waited for Omar. As sophisticated and well dressed people moved around the lobby, we examined them carefully, and imagined who they were and what their lives were like. Were they Colombian? European? North American? On business or vacation? Or out for an afternoon dalliance? At one point there was a rush of activity at the front door when several stylish people wearing sunglasses came in together, followed by two large luggage carts and what appeared to be a few assistants. They could have been Movie Stars, but, alas, there was no Omar.

To help pass the time, we outlined the entire Dr. Zhivago story. By the time we finished, we had also finished our second drink and were hungry. We ordered sandwiches and one more round of drinks and decided that maybe we weren't going to see Omar Sharif after all. Maybe he had canceled, or maybe he was already in his room. At that point it didn't much matter to anybody so, when we had finished eating and had paid the bill, we all made a last stop at the bathrooms and headed out into the early evening rain. It was time to go home. Without ever laying eyes on Omar Sharif, we now had a connection to him. Whenever there was news about him in the future, I always thought about that day when a group of friends sat in the lobby of the Bogotá Hilton, sipping Brandy Alexanders waiting for Dr. Zhivago. He could have been a member of our group.

When Paul called, we made plans to go to Melgar for the weekend. I had asked Barb if she would come to meet Paul's friend, and she was as happy as I to get out of town to a warm climate. Not to mention having dates.

Melgar And The National Pastime

When the weekend finally arrived, Barb and I were excited about our trip to Melgar. Paul and his friend Richard picked us up at 5:00 Friday afternoon, and we were on the road headed down the mountain before dark. In the fading light we could see the changing topography clearly as the flat plateau quickly turned into rolling hills and then became more mountainous and tropical. The emerald greens of the city became darker, and Paul pointed out the spectacular views of the Andes. You could actually see the paths of earthquakes which carved their way through the land and, in the twilight, see pockets of light where groups of indigenous people were ending their day and going about their evening routines. In the cool, mountain air, I felt sure they would all be wearing ruanas. On the beautiful drive, to my surprise, Paul was becoming a compelling storyteller. He knew a lot about the local culture and kept us entertained for the full two-hour trip. Barb and Richard seemed to get along well and, by all accounts, we were a compatible group. The weekend looked promising and, as we approached the warmer climate, we gradually shed our sweaters and took off our heavy socks.

We arrived in Melgar and went directly to the *casita* that Paul and his friends had rented for the weekend. I never actually saw the town of Melgar: only a few other *casitas* along the road tucked

51

into the jungle. The place we were staying in was more like a small motel than a house. Our *casita* had a swimming pool, four or five bedrooms, shared baths, and a small kitchen at the end of the dormitory-style structure. A covered patio with chairs and tables stretched the length of the building, and this is where we spent most of our time, surrounded by lush foliage.

A young man was working around an outdoor cooking pit, and a couple of young women were close by. Paul explained that they would prepare our meals, the night meals being the big ones, and would help us if we needed anything. I don't know where they came from, especially since I couldn't see any other buildings, but they appeared and disappeared without notice throughout the weekend.

After Barb and I got settled in our room, we moved to the patio for drinks and to meet some of the other people. I had met one couple at Oma's, and another couple were Colombian friends of Paul and Richard. Somebody forgot to bring mixers, and the only available thing we had was peach juice, so vodka and peach juice was what we drank that weekend. We finally sat down to eat about 10:30, after a few other people who were not staying with us had arrived. We had a tasty meal of salad, pasta with a red sauce similar to marinara, and bread. We were all hungry and the dinner was delicious. When we finally turned in for the night, things were very quiet: no city noises, TV or partying neighbors. The only sounds came from a few people talking quietly on the patio, and the jungle with its eerie presence.

The next morning, I was the first one up and went immediately to the pool. The air was pristine, the sky was clear, the water in the pool was frigid, and everything seemed the color of emeralds. The only sounds, again, came from the jungle, and I wondered if whatever was in there was watching me as I was watching it, or them – in their home: for this was surely their home, not mine. I waited intently for some creature to charge or slither out but I never saw anything. Within what seemed like minutes, the young man who had helped with dinner arrived with a pot of coffee and a cup on a tray. There was also sugar, milk and a cloth napkin. I've always been a morning person and love a beautiful and peaceful beginning to the day. That morning, with the cool air, the sunny skies, the verdant surroundings, the melodies from the awakening jungle, and

Colombian coffee, I couldn't imagine my mornings would ever be more exquisite.

Before long, as the others started moving around, the day began unfolding with more food, conversation, a lot of swimming and just lounging around the pool. Fortunately, there was plenty of shade, so, staying out of the brutal midday sun was not hard. Someone brought along a copy of the Charles Manson book about the murders in Los Angeles when Sharon Tate and others were brutally killed. Almost everybody picked it up at some point during the weekend and read a few pages between naps. It was a day of relaxation, companionship, and escape from the rigors of the city, and I could understand why so many Bogotanos came to Melgar. It was rustic and simple, and we had everything we needed.

Around dusk our helpers reappeared to prepare for a barbeque by lighting firewood in the outdoor, inground cooking pit. A "barbeque" here referred usually to beef marinated and cooked on a metal grill over the pit. It definitely wasn't North Carolina barbeque, which was pork, marinated in a vinegar/mustard sauce or a tomato-based sauce and cooked for hours. This barbeque was basted with a sauce of cilantro, garlic, onion and vinegar, and was crusty and charred on the edges. Never much of a beef eater myself, I was surprised at how tasty it was and how much I liked it. I tried not to think about where this cow probably was the day before, especially since I had seen so many slabs of beef still on the hoof in the markets. Along with the beef was salad, potatoes also cooked on the grill, and sweet, fried platanos.

We ate slowly, drank beer that somebody had found during the day, and savored every bite and sip. By the time we had finished, the temperature had dropped and we slipped into sweaters before moving away from the tables. The forty-watt light bulbs and a few candles gave off just enough light to create a cozy, nearly hypnotic ambience. I had known some of these people for less than twenty-four hours and was already comfortable with all of them. I was beginning to look at Paul in a different light. It was a couples' weekend, without a doubt, and only briefly did I wonder if I would be attracted to him, or he to me, back in the States. I wasn't sure.

Sunday morning was a repeat of Saturday, with coffee and solitude by the pool, but this time Paul was with me. Our plan was to leave by noon since he had to be at the airport by three o'clock. Before long, Barb and Richard were also up, and we were all getting our suitcases ready for the trip back to Bogotá. We swam a little, ate, showered and packed our bags. After saying goodbye to the others, we started our trek to the city. Barb and I had a lot of schoolwork to do when we got back and leaving a little early suited everybody.

Patricia and friends in Melgar, 1975.

About five minutes out of Melgar we got behind a bicycle race that was heading in the same direction we were. Two police cars were escorting the group and blocking the road, so that neither cars nor buses were able to pass. Ordinarily, a male Colombian driver would be shaking his fist, yelling obscenities, and trying to drive over the curb if he couldn't pass. But the Colombians have such great respect and admiration for sports and young people that the whole scenario evolved into a huge celebration. The cars were traveling four or five abreast (buses included) in one direction, and it was as hot as it can only be at noon, two hours down the mountain from Bogotá. People were leaning out of their cars talking to each other, music was blaring: they were sharing food, beers (and who knows what else) and having a rowdy, fun time. I saw Paul's eyes widen as he surveyed the scene, mumbled something under his breath and gripped the steering wheel a little tighter. He, among all of us, knew what was going on and calmly acknowledged that there was no way he could make his flight that afternoon. So, instead of sulking and complaining, he explained to us more about the second most popular sport in Colombia (soccer being the first), as we joined the party and took part in a typical Colombian custom, following the bicyclists. Every now and then we would stop at a roadside stand and find a bathroom. There were plenty of toilets, just no paper, and we hoped our own supply of tissue, which we had learned to carry with us, wouldn't run out before we got home. After stretching our legs, eating an occasional empanada and drinking a beer, we got back in line and continued the celebration. By this time, of course, we had lost sight of the bikers and just floated along with the crowd until finally, we reached the major highway into Bogotá and were able to pass the team and head back into the city.

The trip took four and a half hours, and Barb and I had been the recipients of a major lesson in patience and the "mañana" philosophy that allowed Paul and the rest of us to keep our cool and make the best of what could have been a very unpleasant situation. I don't remember getting any school work done that Sunday evening, but it was the beginning of a practice that served me well for a long time to come--putting in extra time on Thursday nights so that I could enjoy every minute of the weekend.

There were other trips to Melgar, with nights as soft and irresistible as sinking one's head into a soft down pillow. I knew that I was lucky to have someone to date, and these opportunities to escape the city. Even if I wasn't in love with Paul, I did like him a lot, and I was extremely grateful for the adventure.

Tight Underwear And The President's Palace

With October passing quickly, the import teachers were all thinking about the Christmas holidays and where we were going. Several people were looking into trips within the country, such as Cartagena on the coast, and San Agustin, the most important archaeological zone in Colombia. Others were going to islands in the Caribbean, and one colleague was headed to Argentina. Dot was staying in Bogotá because of the difficulty in traveling with an adopted child, and along with a few others, I was going to the States to visit family and friends. I missed my family and knew I would have the rest of my life to travel, but wouldn't have forever to be with them so, at that time, spending this holiday with them was my priority.

Before any of us could make definite plans to travel outside the country, we had to apply for our *Paz y Salvo,* which was a declaration stating that we had paid our taxes to the Colombian government. Again, the school provided all the support we needed and guided us through the tedious process, which included trips on our own to DAS. With that process in motion, we were free to start making reservations and spent several afternoons at Aviatur, the government- controlled travel agency. Jerry and I seemed to end up together often on these trips into the city and always stopped for something to eat. It never occurred to me, with all the walking we were doing, that I might need to rein in my sampling of the local cuisine, but that awareness came soon enough.

By this time, I was receiving a lot of mail from home and welcoming every letter from my parents, aunts and uncles, friends, and the occasional letter from my two sisters. People I hadn't had contact with in years who found out I was living in Colombia suddenly wrote, curious about my life in this place far from home. My two sisters were busy with their lives, Sara and her four children settling into their new home in Whiteville, and Rachel, in New Bern working on her master's degree while teaching full time. Bobby, the friend I left behind and missed also, was enjoying being back in Whiteville and working in a new medical practice. He was making plans to visit Bogotá, and I was looking forward to showing him the city. My cousin Dave wanted to visit in December, so I was thinking about activities he would enjoy. Mother and Daddy, involved in their retirement activities, were thoroughly enjoying having their four grandchildren so close. All seemed well, and I was getting excited about making the trip home and seeing family and friends.

Around this time, I began to notice that my underwear was getting a little tight, not just snug or out of shape from the hand washing on the scrub boards but literally, too tight. Could I have gained that much weight? I recognized that for one's underwear to be tight one would have to puff up more than what happens with PMS or an extra cookie or two. There was a year in college when I got a little plump, but other than that, weight had never been an issue for me, and I was horrified. We were told that gaining or losing a lot of weight could be one of the signs of a difficult cultural adjustment, and it was then I recognized a need for a huge correction in my eating habits. When I looked at what I had been doing, I was shocked that I had let myself put on these extra pounds.

At that time in Colombia, there were no low-fat foods, diet drinks, or artificial sweeteners. Every time I drank coffee, I used sugar: when out with friends it was beer, wine or Coke with all the food we were sampling because water was not always safe: with sandwiches, I used real mayonnaise, and because I didn't like the taste of the milk, I ate ice cream instead. After school we spent time in the outdoor cafes drinking coffee and tasting freshly baked breads or desserts: followed by a return home to a nice hot meal prepared by Selena. The whole lifestyle sneaked up on me, and by the time I became aware of it, I had gained twenty pounds.

Wrestling with that twenty pounds was frustrating and seemed to be a losing battle. I tried everything, including diet pills, but nothing worked for very long. The pills kept me awake, and, after a while, I realized I needed my sleep more than I needed to lose weight. It wasn't until I later went home for Christmas that the pounds started dropping off, without any real effort on my part, and I wondered about the reason. Here I was, doing what I wanted to do, or so I thought, and struggling with a weight issue. Jerry laughed, (he had lost weight), and said it was the altitude, which I didn't think was very funny. He couldn't understand my concern and thought I shouldn't worry. From that point on I didn't gain any more, but wondered what was happening and was always thinking about the extra pounds.

The school-sponsored activities for the new teachers continued, and we were soon invited to the President's Palace for a tour before the Christmas holidays. It's not open to the public, so we were grateful that President Lopez' son had attended CNG a few years earlier and that good relations between the school and Palace were established. The only request was that all women had to wear dresses or skirts instead of pants. We complied and shivered our way through a very cold day at school, thinking about the warmth of Melgar. When you're used to wearing pants, hose, socks and a sweater on top of a blouse on top of a t-shirt or camisole, and then put on a dress, you feel like you're half-dressed. It was time to go shopping for an appropriate dress. I'd just never felt anything like the winds that whirled around those mountains, even on windy days in New Bern, walking down the street in a minidress, but I managed to find a dress that would get me through the day at work and then into the Palace.

The palace itself was old and musty but beautifully preserved. The solid wood of the furniture shone, the huge crystal chandeliers sparkled, and the floors were like mirrors. The fabrics at the windows were heavy brocade and the furniture was very formal. Huge oil paintings on the walls were of battle scenes and stern-looking men. We saw Bolívar's bedroom and the room (a different one) where he and his mistress were bedded down when he made his famous escape from the window. Shades of Shakespeare! Felipe, the President's son, graciously gave us a personal tour and took us to the President's office where we, naturally, were hoping to meet him. Unfortunately, he was in a staff meeting in the next room. Or so we were told.

While watching the changing of the guard, I couldn't help but compare the U.S. military and the crispness of their dress uniforms with these young men whose clothes didn't fit well and, in some cases, didn't even appear to be part of their uniform. The state of the economy was evident in the shabby uniforms they wore, which contrasted sharply with the opulence of the Palace, and I thought of the high unemployment rate and the half of the population under the age of twenty. Several of the guards slouched and seemed to have little pride and none of the presence of our soldiers. There was a kindness in their eyes but sadness, too. I'd never seen a member of the U.S. military in full dress uniform who wasn't a perfect physical specimen, and I had just taken for granted that any person in the military representing their country was unquestionably at their best. Without wanting to be critical of these young men, I acknowledged a big difference and thought about what went into the disciplined training of the troops back home. Another contrast that made an impression.

Before leaving, a small military band played, first, the Colombian national anthem, a majestic, beautiful song, and then our own national anthem. I don't think I'd ever been moved so strongly by The Star-Spangled Banner, but that day I felt a sense of pride in my heritage I didn't know I had. It was almost like hearing the song for the first time, and I couldn't begin to fathom the meaning of the flag-burning episodes in the last decade in the United States and how nonchalant I had been. I immediately questioned my attitude during those turbulent times and wondered how I could have taken it all for granted so easily. Every time I heard our national anthem after that, I listened in a different way and felt a deeper relationship with my country.

Our hosts were kind and courteous, and the tour of the Palace was another privilege that opened more doors of understanding between our two nations.

The trip back was subdued until someone reminded everybody that Halloween was coming soon, and a big party was being planned – costumes and all. In Colombia, Halloween was a big celebration and mainly for adults, but, before that happened, I had to visit the Doctor and spend a very Catholic night in the hospital.

Hospital Trip

"What's that," Paul asked, as his hand seemed to zero in on a spot on my scalp. We were lounging by the pool, nearly asleep, when he discovered a lump on the top of my head. His hand had been gently caressing my neck and temples, and I was a little annoyed at the sudden intrusion. Somewhat begrudgingly, I felt the spot and noticed for the first time that there was indeed something there that I hadn't felt before. Not overly alarmed, I promised to get it checked as soon as we returned to Bogotá, and then continued with my siesta.

The next day at school I spoke to the nurse, and, after examining what turned out to be a cyst, she recommended I see Dr. Samper, on call for school personnel. When school was over the next afternoon, a school employee drove me across town to his office. Expecting a nondescript, professional looking building similar to ones back home, I was pleasantly surprised to see something altogether different. His office was in a sprawling, stately, colonial home in downtown Bogotá, a home that had been in Dr. Samper's family for generations. The grounds were lush and verdant with wrought iron-benches scattered throughout the gardens, and I immediately wondered if the Spanish conquistadores had ambled along these cobblestone paths. The house had to be full of stories. Was it here three hundred years ago? Perhaps there was a different, smaller structure that had grown to this magnificent edifice with each generation. Soldiers would have found the area more beautiful than anything in Spain. There was just enough afternoon sun to make the trees, recently drenched in a downpour, glisten, and I was so enthralled that all I wanted was to sit down and absorb this fantasy world I was creating.

With my appointment approaching, I didn't linger, but hoped I could come back and explore. The entrance to the office was down a narrow path to a small door at the back of the house. Inside, there were creaky hardwood floors, narrow staircases, tiny windows with only slivers of sunlight shining through, and nurses dressed in starched white uniforms with little caps. I had seen pictures of nurses who looked like this. As I climbed the stairs to Dr. Samper's office, directed by a very formal and professional receptionist, I noticed religious pictures on the walls-Jesus, Mary, heavenly cherubs, crucifixes, and religious sculptures sitting on tabletops. Never had I been to a doctor's office and seen religious pictures like this and immediately felt out of place. Colombia was a Catholic country, and I recognized symbols of their faith, but my experience with anything Catholic on a personal level was limited. Separation of Church (Catholic) and State was all I knew.

When I was growing up, I don't remember knowing anybody who was Catholic. My hometown did have a small Catholic Church, and if ever mentioned, it was always done quietly as if someone wanted to avoid talking. Certainly, my parents never openly discriminated, but my understanding of different religions was sorely lacking; I had never heard much about Catholicism, or Judaism. Growing up I did have Jewish friends, but I just thought of them as members of another Protestant church, like Presbyterian or Episcopalian. In time, of course, my education covered the major religions of the world and other cultures, but, for a long time, seeing religious icons in any place outside of a church seemed unusual. So, coming face to face with my Catholic doctor in these Catholic surroundings was a little surprising.

When Dr. Samper arrived, I was curious, of course. I probably expected the worst, but almost immediately, he put me at ease. His daughter, Charlotte, whom I had met briefly, was a guidance counselor at CNG, and so he knew who I was. He was kind, friendly, and very distinguished. His English was excellent. I knew the school would not send me to anyone with less than stellar qualifications, so I quickly relaxed and tried to ignore the heavenly influences gazing from the walls.

After examining the knot on my head, Dr. Samper rather quickly identified a cyst and was convinced it was benign. He said it should be lanced and then biopsied, and to do that I should plan an overnight stay at the hospital. He quickly scheduled a date and time for the surgery. As I left his office, I was thinking more about the beautiful house than the cyst and hoped I might have a chance soon to see more of it.

After arranging for substitutes at school, Jerry and I set out early in the morning on the day of the surgery; he was taking a day off to go with me. This time, the hospital looked like hospitals I was familiar with, and we quickly went about getting registered and settled in my room. The halls were spotless and the room pristine. Other than the cross above the bed, it could have been in any well-maintained hospital in the States. I was a little surprised Dr. Samper wanted me to spend the night, but I didn't mind and was curious about the experience, and besides, I didn't consider the procedure overly risky.

Soon a nurse came in with a tray full of medical supplies so Jerry took that as his cue to leave. She was a heavyset woman with a kind face and an air of exuberance and energy. I felt immediately at ease. After we greeted each other, in Spanish, she pulled up a chair beside the bed.

"G$sk8J# Lp;s#?," she said.

"What?" I replied.

"Kct3#c*?" she asked again.

This exchange went on a few more times until finally I told her I didn't understand.

"Ah, OK". She quickly pulled out a razor, pointed it in the direction of my head, lifted both hands, palms up, as if to ask, "Where is the cyst?" I immediately understood and showed her where the thing was. It hadn't crossed my mind that she would need to shave the spot, and I was a little shocked. Too late to back out now, I thought, and watched her, very efficiently prepare her tools and then my scalp. She pulled up a big section of hair, cut it with scissors, and then applied an ointment. Next came what sounded and felt like shaving cream and then, very quickly, the razor gently and painlessly pulled across my scalp. Before I knew it, the procedure was over and she was smiling and chatting and putting her things away. When she left, she indicated that someone would soon take me to the operating room. While waiting, I couldn't resist touching the shorn spot with my fingers and was surprised that it felt as smooth as my legs after shaving. The spot seemed to be a little bigger than a half-dollar.

The surgery itself was successful and without incident. When Dr. Samper came in later in the evening, he said the cyst was benign. He told me not to wash my hair for a few days because of the stitches and to rest, and he would see me next week.

Taking pain medication, I had no trouble sleeping that night. The attentive nurses were in and out of my room all night, and I felt comfortable and well-cared for. A heavenly vision of the Virgin Mary holding a cross like the one above my bed floated through my dreams. The only lasting side effect of my hospital visit was a permanent cowlick above the stitches, on top of my skull, which I have to this day.

After a few days of rest, I was out of the apartment and back to work. My first outing was to the apartment of two of the teachers in our group for a Sunday afternoon gathering called *"onces,"* similar to a combination of an afternoon tea and cocktail party. They served *tinto* (the strong, espresso-like coffee), *sabajon* (similar to egg nog and flavored with aguardiente), and many different *pasabocas* (hors d'oeuvres). Everybody wanted to hire my friend's maid! At our first get-together in a month, we had fun talking about our new experiences-not to mention showing off the Spanish we'd learned. We promised to continue getting together as a group since we had already learned how easy it was to lose touch- even though we were working at the same school.

Our Halloween party, at Barb's apartment, was a fun night of outrageous costumes. Those who dressed up did so with style and exuberance. Terry, our redheaded principal, came dressed as a Russian Cossack. His long, orange tunic was belted below the waist with epaulets on the shoulders, the pants were full and fell just below the knee, and a black tassel adorned his red pill box hat. He was quite the dashing military man. His wife wore a long black skirt with rows of trim at the hem, a white peasant blouse, and a saucy hot pink hat with a wide brim. Ed, the man Sarah had been spending a lot of time with recently, must have brought his costume from the States. His clown's outfit was perfect, down to the makeup – mustard-colored baggy pants, a gray and blue long sleeved striped shirt, a purple vest, and a big fuchsia tie that bounced around his chin. His huge white shoes laced up to his ankles. His face was also white with black exaggerated eyebrows and a tear on one cheek, and his smiling lips were fuchsia like his tie. A snappy beret sat on his tousled black curls.

Everybody had thrown together as many bizarre pieces of clothing as he or she could find. One of the most creative was Ernesto, a tall young man in a long diaphanous, pink skirt, navy tank top, flowing flowered scarf around his neck, and a wide-brimmed straw hat. Dark sunglasses completed his outfit. After a few hours of partying, on an unusually warm night in Bogotá, Ernesto took off his hat and sunglasses, put his regular glasses on, and showed off his nearly bald head. He danced more than anybody.

There were a mini-skirted waitress in go-go boots, a good attempt at Mickey Mouse by a petite Asian female, and a very convincing little Bo Peep. It was one of our best parties yet, with good music and good food and a lot of laughter.

As we began to sense the coming holiday season, this party made us think seriously about Thanksgiving and Christmas. In fact, Terry told us that night that Colombia had no turkeys, so someone would try to bring one from the States for our Thanksgiving dinner at Les Landers' house. I had no idea how that could be accomplished since it was absolutely forbidden to bring fresh food, especially meat, into Colombia but acknowledged that if there was a way to get a turkey through Customs, CNG would do it. We were well on our way to the half-way point of our school year, and many of us were getting ready to spend our first Thanksgivings away from our families.

Custom-Made Cape

From the very beginning, my curiosity about foreign cultures included a desire to know how the Colombian people went about their lives on a daily basis. What was ordinary for them? How did family members interact and, especially, how did women of my generation view male/female relationships and careers? I was always surprised by the similarities and accepted the differences, I hope, with fairness and graciousness. Fortunately, at school many Colombian teachers and support personnel seemed to be just as curious about us, the import teachers, as we were about them. One teacher, in particular, was responsible not only for new additions to my wardrobe but also my unique view inside a typical, upper-middle class family.

Nancy Ortiz lived close to the school with her husband Ricardo and four young sons. I was never quite sure what kind of business Ricardo was in, and I rarely saw him, but they lived in a comfortable, well-furnished house on the curving road leading up to the school. Like the grounds at school, lush vegetation covered their property with English Ivy climbing the front of their stone-and-stucco house with colorful flowers artfully placed in the garden. There were cobblestone paths and wrought-iron fixtures on the front door and entryway.

Many houses in Bogotá, especially on the side of town being developed up the mountain, had basements, and the Ortiz family had one that rivaled, in size, all the apartments I had ever lived in. This basement, however, was not a den or family room like many in the States, but a sanctuary for Nancy and her husband. A king-size bed (I hadn't yet seen one of those in Colombia), commanded attention the moment one entered the room. The bed linens were silk and plush with pillows of different sizes and designs carefully arranged on the bed. The headboard appeared to be hand-carved mahogany and towered over the bed. The dominant color in the room was a rich, golden hue, not the brown, tan and burgundy I was accustomed to seeing in other Colombian homes. Across from the bed was a fireplace, surrounded by cream- and pink-toned stone, that was always lit when we were there. Family photos in silver frames were on the mantle. Heavy draperies covered the windows, oil paintings hung on the walls, a stereo with speakers sat on a table, and a small wet bar was tucked into an alcove. No native artifacts adorned the walls as in our apartment. Close to a window were two comfortable chairs with a small table between them, which was a beautiful spot to sit with the sun piercing the thick, glass windows. I was used to seeing the metal bars on windows, and they no longer detracted. The bathroom was also luxurious and large. Blue, white and gold hand-made tiles covered the floor and walls. The spacious shower was built with a partition about five feet tall separating it from the rest of the space so that no shower curtain was needed. It and the separate bathtub were also tiled. In addition, there were two sinks, a commode, a bidet and warm, flattering lighting. Plush towels hung on shiny, brass racks. The basement was all very formal but comfortable.

In this beautiful area Nancy entertained her friends, and we spent several afternoons talking, drinking coffee, and becoming friends. I could often hear the boys upstairs running around and talking to the maids. Occasionally, they would come to the room and knock before entering. The boys were lively and friendly, and the maid was quiet and respectful. This was without a doubt the most sophisticated house I had visited in Colombia.

Nancy was about thirty-five at that time and had made commercials for the local TV station when she was younger. As she started having her children, her jobs changed from the ingénue roles to the young mother and housewife parts. She had started teaching at CNG when her boys were all old enough to start school, but she still did the occasional commercial.

Nancy and I talked about everything: school, men, our families, and clothes. We never discussed politics. Nancy wore fashionable clothes that I admired. One day in the school cafeteria when we were talking about food, I mentioned my weight gain and the need to buy some new clothes. She immediately told me about her seamstress who could make anything if she just had a picture. And not only that, but Nancy also offered to take me to a store to buy fabric and then to the seamstress's house. And so began my glimpse into the daily life of a typical privileged Colombian woman.

On the day we went to the fabric store, her husband's driver picked us up after school and drove us across town to a small shop. Nancy had a beautiful wool cape with fur around the hood, and I decided that would be the first thing I would ask the seamstress to make - without the fur. My ruana was fine for most things, but occasionally I needed a dressier coat. For the cape, I chose a dark blue, light-weight wool material which would be lined in a matching silk, and dark burgundy wool for a skirt. Nancy knew exactly how much fabric to buy, so we quickly made our purchase and returned to the car where the driver was waiting. The cost of my new clothes, including the fabric and seamstress, was $20 US.

Notable to come out of my experiences with Nancy was the awareness that safety issues dictated the lives of many people (women, especially) in Bogotá. Nancy, who didn't drive, depended on her husband (who didn't drive much), and drivers from his business to take her everywhere. She never rode the public buses, as I did, and only rarely used a taxi. Her husband feared for her to be out alone, or with her children, in the car, even in the daytime. Whether the concern had anything to do with her husband's business I wasn't sure. Would she have driven and ventured out on her own if there had not been the safety issue? I don't know. Having the freedom to drive and ride buses was vital to my well-being, and while I enjoyed the luxury of having someone drive me around, I couldn't imagine ever being confined to a life that didn't include a car whenever I needed to go somewhere. Driving myself *did* mean freedom to me.

Nancy and other Colombian women in her social and economic class were curious about the women's rights movement in the States, the sexual revolution, the birth control pill, and job equality.

We talked a lot about the roles of men and women in relationships and how a relationship changes when a woman marries and becomes dependent on her mate, as she was. Typical of all cultures, her married life was based on traditions – traditions that were beginning to fall by the wayside as the social upheavals in the US were felt around the globe. Nancy was questioning everything about her marriage and knew that not every woman relied on her husband as much as she did. It's important to mention here that many women in Colombia were educated, accomplished, and quite capable of providing a good life for themselves. There were more female doctors than male, more female attorneys than male, and the majority of them had attended prestigious universities in the States or Europe. Most of these women, however, when they returned to Colombia, entered into marriages where the husband was unquestionably the lord and master of the household, and the rules would be slow to change. The social/economic class one belonged to didn't matter, and equality between the sexes didn't seem to exist in marriages.

In our own little group of import teachers, we joked about the good life one of our American guys would have if he married a Colombian woman and what a difficult life our women would have with a Colombian husband. We had seen both, and that was our unanimous consensus. To be fair, however, we acknowledged we didn't know a lot of Colombian couples and it was possible not all marriages were like that.

The Ortiz family employed two full-time maids and a gardener to help around the house. With four boys under the age of ten and no washing machine, one maid spent most of her time taking care of the clothes and the other cooked, cleaned, and kept an eye on the boys. In our apartment the maid washed on Mondays, hung clothes out to dry for a day or two, and then started ironing. I could only imagine the amount of work that went into Nancy's maid's life. Nancy was hoping to get a washing machine soon, but there was no guarantee unless they could buy it on the black market. Buying what you needed was not always easy, and just being able to afford something didn't mean you could have it.

Nancy was a loving and devoted mother but I sensed that she longed for more, and the more time I spent with her, the more I knew she was thinking about what she would accomplish when her children were gone. She rarely mentioned her husband, so I can only guess at their relationship. She was definitely in a state of transition, and I'm grateful that she welcomed me so warmly into her home and trusted me enough to share her thoughts and to seek my opinions. Her openness and honesty allowed me an insight into a Colombian woman's life that I may have missed if we hadn't become friends. With some people you meet, you feel an immediate connection, and she was that kind of person to me. Our obvious cultural similarities and differences only enhanced our friendship. Nancy became a dear, respected friend. In years to come, whenever I would wear the cape, I would think about Nancy and her life in Colombia, a life filled with maids and drivers, exquisite handmade clothes, and the constant fear for her own and her family's safety, a life so different from mine but full of similar dreams and hopes for the future.

First Party And Thanksgiving

As the teachers took turns entertaining in our apartments on Friday nights, we were developing patterns. Because transportation at night was difficult and only the local teachers had cars, we would sometimes sleep over at the hosts' apartment. It was a practical way of dealing with night-time activities, and some people even brought their sleeping bags to avoid sleeping on hard floors. So, when it came our time to host the party, we cleaned everything and tried to find comfortable places for people to sleep. We had plenty of space in the apartment but not a lot of furniture. Dot and I each had a single bed and a third bed for Lucía, but, since she slept in a crib, that one extra bed served as our guest bed and we could also use the sofa. Two chairs facing each other could pass for a bed, and that was about it. Anybody who wanted to spend the night and didn't end up in one of those places had to sleep on the floor.

The biggest challenge for our parties was planning the food. With a tiny refrigerator, we weren't able to make things ahead of time and store them, and we certainly didn't have space to freeze anything. We looked for food that didn't need refrigeration and started grocery shopping a few days before the party. We bought chips, cheese, meat that reminded me of Hickory Farms beef logs, extra mustard, some beer and wine. Preparing gourmet dishes was out of the question. Fortunately, most people brought snacks and something to drink, but they didn't always know ahead of time what they would bring so, we could have ended up with twenty bags of chips. It never happened, but it could have. Our good fortune was having a maid who was happy to make empanadas on the day of the party and also mushrooms stuffed with cheese and bread crumbs. She also cleaned and sliced some celery and carrots. Our guests were not picky.

People started arriving around 9:00 p.m. and before long the food, drink and music had everybody in a good mood and dancing. What an assortment of dancers! Our Colombian friends tried to teach us to Salsa. None of us had much luck, but it didn't matter. We did our own Salsa and even tried the Cumbia again. After a fun night, at 2 a.m. the last guest who was leaving, left. Those remaining found their sleeping spots and were dead to the world in no time.

Around 7 o'clock the next morning, I woke up to what sounded like pots and pans being tossed around. I stumbled to the kitchen and found Selena, who seemed exasperated, trying to clean and put things away. The living room and kitchen were disaster areas. There was uncovered food on the tables and the floor, empty coke, beer and wine bottles, half- filled glasses, paper plates and napkins everywhere.

With nearly everybody smoking, the ashtrays were overflowing. If I had been thinking of asking for breakfast, I quickly decided against that and realized that all I needed to do was get out of her way and send home those people who were stretched out on the floor in the living room. I woke them all up and got them out of the apartment as quickly as possible. At that point there was nothing left to do but go back to bed and try not to bother Selena. I stopped by Dot's bedroom to let her know what was going on and then crawled into my bed and went back to sleep.

When I finally got up again, it was after noon, and the apartment was spotless. Dot, who was waiting for me to stir, and I crept very cautiously into the kitchen, apologized for the mess, thanked Selena for cleaning everything, and told her we were going out. She didn't speak any English, but we could almost hear her berate those *crazy* Americans! Dot and I returned in time for dinner and what Selena prepared for us was our least favorite meal – rice, pasta, and salad, and that was all. We expected it, ate it, and tried to be properly remorseful. The next day, she was feeling much better, and our meals soon improved.

It was a great party and typical of many that year. There's no doubt that most of us were attending more parties here in Bogotá than we ever did back home. The need to connect with friends was strong.

I was hearing from my family and friends on a regular basis and always looked forward to news from home. In fact, I had just seen a newspaper article in the Bogotá paper, El Tiempo, about the fishing boat "Lillian B," full of Colombian marijuana, which had landed in the port of Beaufort, very close to New Bern. Nine Colombians were arrested, according to the article, so I was beginning to get hometown news from the local newspaper as well as letters from home. A few former colleagues and friends from Whiteville and New Bern also wrote, and I was maintaining ties to my life back in the States and often missed home. My cousin Dave was planning to visit in December, and after Christmas Bobby and I were scheduling a trip to San Andrés, a small island off the coast of Nicaragua. He was coming with me to Bogotá for a few days after our New Year's holiday, so I was busy trying to organize everything and make reservations. My schedule for the trip home was long with changes in Miami and Atlanta before arriving at the Raleigh-Durham airport around 9:30 p.m. I found no convenient flight into Myrtle Beach or Wilmington, so, again, my parents volunteered to pick me up and take me back to Whiteville.

With all of the excitement about holiday travel, Thanksgiving was another opportunity for us to be festive. CNG honored the major American holidays and, to make sure we didn't have time to get homesick, scheduled a Thanksgiving dinner on Thursday. We were looking forward to celebrating with our friends and trying to recreate some familiar dishes. For the dinner at Les and Marcia Landers' house (he was the high school principal), Les would cater the meat, (there was still some uncertainty about the turkey), and all guests would bring dishes. Casseroles made with canned soups were out of the question, so we concentrated on what we could make with the available ingredients.

On Thanksgiving morning Jerry and Matt showed up at our apartment early to make deviled eggs. I was taking potato salad, and Dot was taking a rice dish. With a little help from Selena, we pulled it all together and set out, with Lucía and her diaper bag, for the Landers' house. We ended up taking two taxis since we couldn't all fit in one and arrived ten minutes apart.

When we walked in the Landers' door, there was no mistaking the aroma of a basted, cooking turkey. I could smell the butter, onions, celery, and spices and knew that somebody had managed to smuggle the bird through Customs. Long tables in the living area were already full of a variety of bowls and plates with appetizing food. We added our contributions to the array and joined our colleagues. Most of us sat on the floor and drank sangría full of fresh pineapple, oranges, and other fruit. Not long after, Bruce started playing jazz selections on the upright piano, which surprised all of us because we didn't know he could play. When he broke into a rousing rendition of Gershwin's "Rhapsody in Blue," we were astonished. He had a professional-caliber talent and we were simply amazed. He continued for about thirty minutes of nonstop music. The happy tone had been set, and everybody floated along on the high that good music brings.

Late in the afternoon Les announced that the turkey was ready, and we gathered for the meal. Not only did someone manage to get a turkey, they also managed to bring some aluminum foil-unavailable to us at the time-to wrap it in. After Les offered a blessing, all of us gave our own silent thanks for this special occasion, here with our friends, in the midst of our personal journeys. With overloaded plates we found places to sit and enjoyed the lovingly prepared dishes. The children in the group, who added so much to our experience, were well-behaved and enjoyed the day and food as much as the adults. After trips back to the table for seconds, we stretched our legs and walked around a bit before desserts and coffee. Movelle made a mock apple pie (we rarely had access to apples) that tasted like the real fruit. Somebody else made a tasty rhubarb pie (which I had only heard of). Spice cakes, a rum cake, and chocolate brownies filled our plates.

We talked about the upcoming holidays and everybody's destinations. We arranged to take those who needed transportation to the airport, and talked about the plans for those who were staying in Bogotá. I was content.

While sitting on the floor in the living room after the sumptuous meal, I couldn't help but notice the clothes we were all wearing as I tried to capture the scene in my mind. Les was elegant and fashionable in a white turtleneck sweater, plaid pants, smoking his pipe. Jerry was wearing a western-style shirt with jeans, Dot had on lavender pants and a purple sweater, and Marcia, Les' wife, was wearing a flowered baby-doll dress. Bruce had on a long-sleeved striped shirt with turned-up sleeves for playing the piano and a navy vest, his wife Movell, a red turtleneck sweater and jeans, and I was wearing a patchwork blouse over a dark blue t-shirt and bell-bottom jeans. Nearly all of us were wearing Colombian boots. The children were dressed in jeans and t-shirts and sneakers. There was a cozy fire, the afternoon light was dim, we were smoking, and even the kids were talking quietly. It was our family reunion. Our ruanas were scattered around the room, as well as our backpacks; there was food and coffee nearby. Whenever I try to picture a scene in my mind that portrays the essence of our experience in Bogotá, it is always that Thanksgiving afternoon that comes to mind.

We left late in the day, before dark, just as a heavy downpour came through. We each probably spent a quiet and mellow night, lulled by the rain and a sense of reflection.

Cousin Dave And The Women

Like children we were making our Christmas lists as we planned our trips home for the holidays. Almost greedy, we thought about many things we didn't have in Bogotá that we would certainly find at home. I missed cheddar cheese, peanut butter, succulent seafood, creamy white sauces laced with sherry, milk, grits, chocolate chips, walnuts for cookies, and dried salad-dressing mixes.

On my list to bring back with me were things I could get through Customs. I wanted panty hose (with nude heel and toe), underwear, Estee Lauder foundation in Country Beige, skin care products, Le De by Givency, Bain de Soleil suntan lotion, Avon's Skin so Soft, which was a great mosquito repellant, and personal hygiene products. At my parents' house I had stored clothes I didn't think I would need in Bogotá, such as shorts I could wear in Melgar and coats for days when neither my ruana nor my cape were right, electric hair rollers, and small kitchen appliances. I was looking forward to going through all of that. Dot's blender had blown out, and the repair bill would have been 800 pesos, more than the cost of a new one, and we really used the blender a lot. Selena used it to make our fruit juices, soups and sauces so that was definitely on my list.

At the top of my list for things to do was to drive somebody's car through the North Carolina countryside, to be in control behind the wheel for a while. I wanted to see the beach again with its wide strand, and the gray-white sand that wasn't full of rocks, visit with relatives at the beach and in Raleigh, and drive to New Bern to see friends. I wanted to babysit my nieces and nephews, wash my clothes in a washing machine with Downy softener, sleep in a comfortable double bed, not struggle with the language for a while, and go to a movie and eat popcorn. And I also wanted to be surrounded by the quietness that enveloped my parents' house in a grove of pine trees in a small Southern town. Hearing a soft, Southern accent would be nice, too.

As our lists kept growing, we checked in with each other daily to see who had come up with the most outlandish and out-of-the-ballpark wishes.

Leaving Colombia as a registered alien required a lot of paperwork and time. Taxes had to be filed, and paid, and then, after approximately ten days, and only then, could our *paz y salvo* be issued, which allowed us to leave the country. Once all of that came through, we were free to make reservations and final plans. It was a busy time. Activities at school also increased as we prepared for exams, parent conferences, and Christmas parties for the students.

In the midst of all of this I received a letter from my cousin Dave saying he would visit soon, and I was thrilled. Dave was a little younger than I, single, and we shared a sense of adventure. The year before, when he, my sister Rachel, and I spent Christmas week in Southern Spain, I found him to be a good traveling companion. I wanted to make sure he met my friends and tasted life in Bogotá. For six days he would have plenty to do. When I showed my friends Dave's picture, they lined up to serve as tour guides.

By December, not many of us had found people to date. We had expected to meet no one special, but it didn't stop us from keeping our eyes open just in case somebody came along. Having a romantic interest, of course, enriched our experience, and those of us who were dating somebody locally, knew we were lucky. For me, going out with Paul when he was in town added another dimension to my life in Bogotá and gave me something to look forward to. I knew it was probably not a relationship that would last beyond my time there, but I was, nevertheless, glad he was around.

So, when Dave showed up, tall, blond, with a mustache and looking like Clark Gable, I became the most popular, sought-after person in our group. All the single women, imports and locals suddenly became my best friends. Before I could plan any activities, they were volunteering to take days off from work to usher him around the city.

The night he arrived, Jerry, Carol (one of the teachers I didn't know well), Josie (who had connections in Raleigh where Dave grew up), and I were waiting for him in the Avianca lobby at El Dorado airport. As usual, it took a long time for him to get through Immigration and Customs. When he finally walked through the gate, he received a rock star's welcome. He must have been shocked at the attention, but I was happy my friends were willing to take the time to welcome him to our city. He was tired from a long day, and it was after 11 p.m. when we arrived back at the apartment. Since the next day was a school day, Dave would sleep in while we worked and everybody could start visiting after school. Welcome!

Selena was as giddy as my friends and seemed eager to help make Dave comfortable. He spoke enough Spanish to get through the next day in the apartment with her and the babies. When Dot and I got home the next afternoon, he was refreshed and ready to go out. The Phelans, the couple with three children, hosted several of us for dinner that night. Dave and I headed out to flag down a taxi, which was not his normal mode of transportation, and had no trouble getting one to stop. Fortunately, there was a break in the weather, and there was no rain in sight.

Among the single teachers, Dave was the center of attention. Carol volunteered to take off the next day, a Friday, and take him to the Gold Museum and other local attractions, and, not surprisingly, he was eager to see the sights. Josie volunteered to be his guide on Monday, and we would all celebrate together over the weekend with a trip to Chía, a small village nearby. To get there would require our riding a public bus for about an hour, and then we'd tour Simón Bolívar's home, which had been beautifully restored. A trip to some of the outdoor markets was on the agenda also, and everything revolved around restaurants and eating local food. Dave's schedule was full, and the ladies were having a great time. Men like Dave were few and far between in our environment and he was experiencing a rarefied view of Colombian life. I told him later that he owed me.

One afternoon, Selena approached me very quietly with a small problem she was having with Dave. He was asking her for a fresh towel every day, and we just didn't have enough for him to use a new one every day. We used our towels for several days since she washed only on Mondays and it took a couple of days for them to dry.

Once I explained the situation to Dave, he understood immediately. I'm not sure why Selena didn't tell him herself, but I think it had to do with the macho society and her concept of her own place in our lives. He, of course, was very gracious to Selena and went out of his way to ease her concerns. I laughed at how accustomed I had become to the washing situation and was grateful it had not been a problem for me, or, for him.

Another day, I came home from work, and Dave, who had been in the apartment a few hours, told me about hearing a noise that sounded like planes flying overhead close by. Concerned, because our apartment was not near the airport, he asked Selena if she knew what it was. She smiled immediately and said, "Futból." Apparently, at a soccer match in a nearby stadium, the enthusiasm of the crowd sounded like the roar of jet engines. It was so common for us that we rarely noticed it.

Dave's days were filled with the sights, sounds, and smells of Bogotá, accompanied by adoring females (and a few males). Whether he made plans to see some of his admirers later in the States, I don't know. But his visit to Bogotá was a small step in creating positive relations between people of two countries who sometimes eyed each other suspiciously. He left with a great deal of respect and admiration for the Colombian people, and I'm sure the people who met him felt the same way. He certainly left behind an adoring and appreciative female entourage.

Dave arrived back in the States before I did, in time for the annual Woodard Christmas reunion, but, unfortunately, I missed it that year. It was one of the few I missed in my entire life.

Home For The Holidays

The days before Christmas vacation in Bogotá were just like days in every American school where I had ever worked. The students and teachers were all excited about the upcoming three-week break, and trying to hold the students' attention and keep them on task was challenging. The upper and lower schools held separate assembly programs on the last day. We sang Christmas carols in English and Spanish and watched several student groups who played rock music and danced. Following the assembly, each grade level returned to its own area for more music, dancing by everyone, and plenty of food. A lot of the parents attended, even in the high school group, and this was when they gave gifts to the teachers. I was embarrassed and overwhelmed to receive such lavish gifts; a hand painted vase by a well-known Colombian artist, very nice Chilean wines, the use of a finca for a weekend, a handmade sweater, delicate porcelain *tinto* cups, and many more exceptional gifts. This vote of confidence made me humble and grateful, and I was determined more than ever to provide the best educational experience possible for my students.

Before I left for North Carolina, Jerry, Matt, Sarah and I attended a performance of the play "Dracula" in which Denise had a nonspeaking role as a maid. She was having a great time with a local theater group. Another teacher who had married a Colombian musician a few years earlier, played the drums with his jazz group, and we had recently attended their concert at the Centro Americano. Teachers were pursuing their own interests, and we supported each other as a family does. This *was* our family, and we all had our places.

On Monday, December 22, Jerry rode to the airport with me. I didn't need any help but I enjoyed his company. He was staying in Colombia during the holidays, and because he didn't have any family to visit in the States, he planned to travel to Cartagena during the break. Dot had wanted to visit Venezuela, but problems with Lucía's papers were keeping them in Colombia. A few other import teachers planned to stay in Bogotá, but most were going away for at least two weeks.

When I walked through the gate and turned around to wave to Jerry, I had the same feeling I'd experienced when I turned to wave to my parents in Wilmington back in August. There's no doubt that I was excited about going home, but I felt a twinge of nostalgia for Colombia already, and I wasn't even out of the airport! But I made it home safely and had no more pangs of sentimentality, for a while.

The holidays were fun and full of activities. I saw friends and family, but I had missed the Woodard reunion. I did see Dunnagan relatives in Myrtle Beach several times. My grandmother liked my cape and noted that I had put on a few pounds. While at the beach, I ate as much seafood as I could. My closest friends in Myrtle Beach, Marilyn and Sam Talbot, were on vacation with their family in London, and I was sorry I missed them. Marilyn and I shared a love of traveling and had taken several trips together and I looked forward to seeing them on my next trip home.

When my college roommate, Linda Callihan, visited one afternoon, we sat by the fire and talked about old and new times. I took trips to the doctor and dentist and it was great to get rid of five months' worth of *tinto* on my teeth. I rummaged through things in the bedroom at my parents' house and packed up some clothes and kitchen gear to ship back. Paul had given me the address of his shipping agent in Miami, so I packed whatever I needed without concern about weight. And, of course, I drove. Mother let me use her car, so I was free to go anywhere I wanted. When I drove to New Bern to visit friends, I felt like a sixteen-year-old just getting her license. Driving was liberating!

Once the Christmas rush was over, Bobby and I spent a lot of time together. The restoration of his house at Lake Waccamaw was finished, and it was a peaceful retreat for us. Because he had sprained his ankle skiing, he would not be returning with me to San Andrés and then Bogotá, but he was able to get around enough that the two of us could spend some time relaxing together and talking. He enjoyed hearing about my Colombian adventures, and I enjoyed sharing them. Other than my Dad, Bobby probably had more interest than anyone. He planned to visit later, once he could walk comfortably. In the meantime, I had to decide whether to go to San Andres alone. We'd had reservations for a month. Since I didn't know when I might be able to go there again, I decided to go ahead with plans to spend a few nights there before going back to Bogotá.

My vacation in Whiteville was over in a flash, and by the time I left home I was ready for the sights and sounds of Colombia again, not to mention the empanadas.

New Years Holiday
In San Andres

Ever my dependable companion and supporter, my Dad drove me to the Fayetteville airport before daybreak on December 30, 1975, and sat with me in the waiting room. I didn't know until much later that he had filmed me with his eight-millimeter camera as I crossed the tarmac wearing my handmade cape and boots from Bogotá. The misty film on that rainy Tuesday morning could have been from the El Dorado airport in Bogotá.

The trip into San Andrés should have been easy, but the flight from Miami was delayed two hours and changed everything. By the time we landed at the small airport, 140 miles east of the coast of Nicaragua, the sun was setting and traffic was sparse. Few people were milling around, and the airport was ready to close for the night. Getting through Customs seemed a chore for everybody. I had hoped for a long hot bath and a seafood dinner in a relaxing tropical hotel, but now the most I hoped for was an air-conditioned room and privacy.

The short ride to the hotel was just long enough for the humidity and warmth to settle on my hair and skin, reminding me of coastal North Carolina in August. The taxi was small, old, with a radio playing full blast and windows that rolled down easily. The driver was friendly and asked why I was in San Andrés alone for the holiday. I told him I was a teacher in Bogotá, returning from a visit with my family in North Carolina, and was just stopping off to see the island. He welcomed me profusely, almost too enthusiastically, I thought, and I was glad to reach the hotel.

Nothing could have prepared me for what happened next. It never occurred to me that there might be a problem with my reservations, or that I could possibly be stranded in the hotel lobby that first night, but that's exactly what happened. A kind, accommodating desk clerk looked at my copy of the reservation, shook his head sadly, and said there was no room available. His English was worse than my Spanish, but he communicated very quickly that there was nothing he could do until the next day. Too exhausted to be angry, and aware that there was nothing to do, I lugged my suitcase over to the nearest chair and sat down.

It was close to 9 p.m. by then, and I was hungry and thirsty. The restaurant in the hotel served only breakfast and lunch, and I didn't want to venture out alone at that time, so the clerk said he would find me something to eat. Soon one of the maids brought me a sandwich with chips and a Coke, one of the best meals I had ever eaten. When I finished, I found a bathroom before settling down for what I knew would be a long night in the lobby. At 10:00 o'clock, the same maid who had brought me the sandwich came back and told me I could go with her to a temporary room for the rest of the night. Hopeful, I followed her to a room, which I found out later was where she and her husband, the night clerk, lived. The room was obviously lived in, but there was a clean bed with fresh sheets and a pitcher of water with a glass by the bed. I didn't bother to change clothes because I was hoping it would be only a matter of hours before I could get to my own room. After closing my eyes for a short while, sure enough, the maid returned, and said my room was ready. I quickly gathered up my things and followed her to the wing where the guests stayed and gratefully thanked her and her husband for their help. When I was finally alone, too tired to be angry or wonder what had happened to the reservation, I fell into the bed and dreamed of coconuts with bowling-ball eyes falling from palm trees.

San Andrés and neighboring Providencia had been settled by English Puritans in 1630 and captured by the Spanish soon after, in 1641. In the early 1800s Spain assigned the islands and Panama and parts of Nicaragua to New Granada, which later became known as Colombia. In 1912 Colombia established a local administrator in the two island groups, which were called the Archipelago of San Andrés y Providencia. Because they were still under Colombian rule at this time, I, with my Colombian resident visa, could visit without special papers.

San Andrés was a quaint and charming island, especially attractive to Colombians who could travel there without paying their taxes before leaving home. Like most Caribbean islands, it possessed a lifestyle that was relaxed and laidback. Not overrun by tourists, it was possible to move around the island safely and visit local spots and meet local people without worrying about exorbitant prices and getting ripped off. Many people rode scooters, and I was looking forward to renting one on the morning of December 31, 1975, New Year's Eve.

After sleeping late that morning and then enjoying a long, hot shower, I stepped out on the patio just outside my room where a few guests were having breakfast. A waitress soon appeared with coffee and took my order, and I glanced around to see what I had missed the night before. The tiled- top tables each had four chairs, and it was possible to see the beach from a few of the tables. On the patio were palm trees and prolific bougainvillea in pots, wet from a recent watering. A small water hose snaked along the gravel as if to protect the garden area from the brutal sun beginning to make a bold appearance. I was grateful I had stocked up on sunscreen when I was home. I was very comfortable and mellow, and other than a brief, unusual sensation in my right eye, everything seemed very normal, and I was glad I had decided to stop over for a few days.

Not long after my fruit, eggs, bread, and coffee arrived, a man approached my table politely and unobtrusively and asked if he could join me. I had not been looking for company, but he seemed harmless enough, and we were in a public place, so I invited him to sit down. Colombians are some of the politest people in the world, and so, when Carlos told me he was from Bogotá, I was not surprised. His family was from the island, and he was visiting for the holiday. He had left when he was a young man just out of high school and gone to the Capital in search of better job opportunities. He worked with an insurance company and had learned to speak

English with clients from the States. He talked about his family: one brother, he said, was the family's last connection to Africa. By that he meant that this brother was the darkest skinned of the clan, and he laughed whole-heartedly when he told me that. I hadn't thought much about having siblings who were different colors, but skin color had a different meaning in Colombia than it did in the States. I hoped he was not trying to shock me or get a reaction regarding race, but I soon realized that wasn't his motive at all. After all, I was surrounded by Colombians, and many of them had African roots. Skin color was just not something I thought about.

I ended up going out with Carlos twice in the next two days. That afternoon we went for a ride around the island on his motorbike and then stopped early in the evening for some local turtle soup in an outdoor restaurant overlooking the water. Even though it was New Year's Eve, I came in early and relaxed in the room and later on the hotel patio.

The next day Carlos and I took a rental boat to a tiny island that could be seen from the shoreline in front of the hotel. People went there to gather shells and walk. With no facilities, no one stayed long, and other than offering a beautiful view of the Caribbean its most compelling attraction was the men in their European-style bikini bathing suits. I was still trying to adjust to those tiny suits.

Without taking too much of my time, Carlos had appeared at just the right moment. He was not demanding, he was good company and very nice-looking, especially in his bathing suit. We made plans to get together in Bogotá after the holidays, and I gave him my phone number.

It had been a good break, but I was ready now to unpack my suitcase and settle into my routine back "home." The desk clerk who checked me in the night I arrived was at the desk when I checked out, and again he apologized for the inconvenience regarding the reservation. I passed it off and thanked him and his wife for their help. I had left a good tip for them in my room. On the way out the front door, I experienced the same sensation in my eye that had appeared the first time on New Year's Day, and, suddenly, I became alarmed. Not now, I thought, I'm not sure how to deal with an eye problem, which could be serious, and I pushed it out of my mind for the time being and headed to the airport.

Medical Emergency

Jerry and Barb were waiting for me at the airport when I arrived, and I was happy to see them. When we all parted ways in early December, we had traded travel schedules, including return flight information, just in case anybody was able to get to the airport to meet anybody else. We were all quite capable of getting from the airport back to our apartments alone, but the "safety-in-numbers" concept was always present, so we volunteered whenever we could. The taxi ride from the airport into the city at night, even with friends, could still be scary. The school also had our information and checked on all of us.

After our breaks, we were ready to slow down and readjust. Jerry was still recuperating from a vicious sunburn he got on the beach in Cartagena, and Barb was happy to have seen friends in Venezuela she had met the year before when she taught there. Dot and Lucía just relaxed in the apartment and explored the city during the break, and Selena and her baby spent time with her family in a nearby town. Sarah reconnected with her boyfriend in Boston. Fortunately, we had several days before school reopened.

We slept late, had leisurely breakfasts, and then made our plans for each day. We did nothing more than eat out in restaurants or sidewalk cafés, visit new sites, and walk around the city. Dot and I talked late in the evenings about our plans for our students in the coming semester and shared ideas about the individualized instruction we were trying to provide. We both had been involved with similar programs in the States and wanted to expand our focus as we went into the second half of the year.

At some point, before we returned to work, I mentioned to Dot the situation with my eye and asked her opinion. She was so levelheaded that I valued her thoughts and, besides, I just needed to share the information because I knew I should not ignore my concern. She very adamantly suggested I see a doctor soon, confirming what I had in mind. As soon as we returned to work, I would ask the school to recommend a specialist.

Soon we were back at our jobs and quickly into our familiar routines. The students were ready to work and seemed eager to tackle new challenges. For the first time, we finally saw Bogotá without the gray, dreary skies and relentless rain: January was beautiful. It still rained, but the showers were short and seemed merely to cleanse the sun-filled sky. The ferocious wind seemed calmer, too.

The school made an appointment for me to see a physician, and one afternoon in mid January Barb and I went to his office. I had written a letter to Bobby, who continued to practice medicine with my family doctor in Whiteville, and wished it were easier to call on the phone. I explained what was going on and asked for suggestions. I knew he would answer my letter, and I was anxious to hear from him, even though I knew he couldn't make a diagnosis through the mail. My vision was definitely blurred in the right eye now with a field cut being the most pronounced symptom and, even though it tended to come and go, it was happening more frequently.

The doctor asked questions, examined me, and said there was a blockage in one of the veins to the retina. Since it was a Friday, he scheduled more tests for the following Tuesday. In the meantime, he told me to avoid heavy lifting and strenuous physical activity. It was an uneasy weekend, but my friends were solicitous, and I knew I would have all the support I needed from the school. I planned to talk to our Director, Phyllis, on Monday during my planning period.

Prior to my planning period on that Monday, Phyllis' secretary came to my room and told me I had a phone call from the States, and I could take it in Phyllis' office. She would keep my class until I could get back. Phone calls through the Director's office for us were very rare and usually foretold of some emergency, so

I immediately thought something had happened to someone in my family. I flew down the hall, into the Administration building and up the stairs to Phyllis' office. She was sitting at her desk, and when I walked in she stood up, smiled kindly and handed me the phone. She then walked out and left me with privacy. It was Bobby on the line, and he immediately told me that everybody was fine, not to worry. International calls were often difficult, and our connection on this one was not good. With the transatlantic delay, also, it was challenging to talk. He was calling about my letter and said he had shown it to my doctor. Both of them were concerned that the eye problem might be a detached retina or something worse. He recommended that I come home immediately for evaluation, and treatment, if necessary, in hospitals he knew. He would send me a ticket if I needed him to. I told him that wouldn't be necessary and that I would call him back after talking to Phyllis.

Gathering my thoughts to tell Phyllis all of this was challenging. Leaving Colombia again, after less than a month, and just coming back from Christmas would not be easy. There was the tax situation, lesson plans, finding a substitute, not knowing how long I would be away and worst of all-what was going on? Was it serious? I had many questions, and I wasn't even convinced that I needed to leave. Why not continue with my scheduled appointment here tomorrow and wait for that diagnosis?

I talked to Phyllis about all of my options, and after nearly thirty minutes and after considering her recommendations, I decided to return to the States for a diagnosis. The school would request emergency medical leave for me and, if granted, would make it possible for me to leave on short notice. They would take care of everything, including canceling the follow-up appointment scheduled for the next day. I called Bobby back from her office, told him I'd let him know as soon as I could when I would be arriving.

Actually getting the necessary clearance to leave the country took about two weeks. During that time of waiting and trying to make plans I found it extremely hard to focus on teaching. The uncertainty of what lay ahead was frightening, and the prospects for my future were unclear.

Finally, when my departure day arrived, my friends took me to the airport. The school had warned me that because of the special leave I received, there could possibly be some delays in going through Immigration and Customs. Not only was the Colombian government concerned about what foreigners might bring into the country, they were also concerned about what was taken out. The first sign that this would not be a typical exit came when I showed my passport and papers for the first time at the check-in desk. After close scrutiny I was ushered behind the counter, through a door, to an area that opened up to offices where serious-looking people were going about their business. Most were in uniforms, and there were a few like me who were tourists just trying to make their flights. Suitcases and bags were being thoroughly searched, and it appeared that body searches were coming. When my turn came, a polite officer spoke respectfully to me, went through everything in my pocketbook and suitcase, said they were looking for drugs, and then told me to follow the female attendant. She led me to a small room where she told me to take off my clothes. I was wearing a belted burgundy corduroy dress over a navy turtleneck sweater, a camisole top, bra, pantyhose, panties, and boots. I thought that surely, I wouldn't have to remove everything, but, other than my panties, that's exactly what she told me to do. The panties had to be pulled down while a complete body search was done. It was probably the most humiliating thing that had ever happened to me in my life, and I felt acutely violated.

Of course, no drugs were found, and I was eventually cleared to board. I couldn't wait to be airborne and smoke a cigarette.

A Lost Month

Was the cause birth control pills, smoking, the altitude, or multiple sclerosis? Maybe none of these things. There was definitely a blood clot behind my optic nerve, which could have indicated many things, but by the end of my four weeks at Duke hospital, all I knew for sure was that I had a loss of vision in the lower left quadrant of my right eye. Every test imaginable had been done, and the only consensus was that I had a form of optic neuritis. No definitive test could diagnose MS, and time would be the only way we would know about that.

At some point during the third week, while I was recuperating from some of the more invasive tests and receiving a week's worth of the hormone ACTH, I asked my doctor about returning to Colombia. How soon did he think I'd be ready to go back? I was feeling fine and wanted to let the school know something. They had been in contact with my family, but I knew they needed to know what to expect for the rest of the semester.

At this time, he told me a little more about the pneumoencephalogram, a test done about a week after I entered the hospital. A small amount of cerebrospinal fluid was drained from the brain and replaced with air, oxygen or helium, which allowed the brain to show up more clearly on an x-ray. It's painful and dangerous and generally not well tolerated by patients. Replacement of the spinal fluid is by natural generation and requires a recovery period of 2-3 months before normal movement is restored. Yes, it was very painful, and I was on my back for a couple of weeks and stiff for a long time. My sister Rachel took a week off from work to stay with me since I needed help doing the most basic things. Because of this test and the recuperation period, and also, because the steroids could weaken my immune system, making me vulnerable to infection, Dr. N recommended that I resign. Maybe by April, he said, I could return to Colombia to pack up my things and bring them back. In the meantime, he thought I should rest and regain my strength. He would determine later, after regular follow-up visits, when it would be safe to travel again.

I was floored. My most pressing need was to contact the school that I could not return, and I sent a letter immediately. As usual, CNG was concerned and supportive, and indicated they were anxious to hear from me again.

After four weeks in Durham, my dad picked me up and took me to Whiteville. The month of March and most of April I spent relaxing, gaining my strength back and thinking about this most recent experience. While everybody else was working, I was enjoying a beautiful spring, reading a lot, writing letters, and looking for direction. I felt sadness and disbelief, as well, at this turn of events and a great sense of loss, but I was holding on to a dream that wasn't over yet. Bobby was attentive, and I knew how lucky I was to have this wonderful family and devoted friends. I was feeling strong and healthy, and each visit with Dr. N left me feeling good about the future. Finally, he gave me the OK to return to Colombia to pack up my things, and I made reservations immediately.

¡Ciao, Colombia!

If there was a natural remedy for improving my health at that time, it was the return trip to Colombia. I could have arranged for my things to be returned, but I needed to make the trip myself. It was important that I take some responsibility, and even though my funds were dwindling, I chose to make the trip. I was thrilled to be going back and looked forward to seeing everybody. With mixed emotions about the job, I thought, of course, about returning to work and finishing out the year. But that decision was made when I put my faith in Dr. N and accepted his recommendation that I resign. In time, that was a decision I questioned profoundly, but now, I was on my way and was determined to see and do everything I possibly could in the two weeks I needed to settle my affairs.

Left to right, Denise, Patricia, Jerry, Barb and
Sarah at El Dorado airport, Bogotá, 1976.

Several of my friends met me at the airport with flowers and
champagne, and after taking a few pictures and picking up my bags,
we headed to the car that Sarah had recently bought. It was a warm
welcome, and I was greatly appreciative of their effort.

The first order of business was to visit the school the next
day and talk to Terry, my principal, and Phyllis. There would be
a lot of paperwork to do to get my *Paz y Salvo* again and end my
contract. Getting clearance would take at least two weeks under the
circumstances, so that was the most urgent matter.

That morning, after visiting my students and the business
office, Terry asked me to come to his office. He was kind and
considerate and asked if I would consider staying for the remainder
of the term, which was about two more months. Not realizing that I
truly had a choice, I said I should do what my doctor recommended,
which was to resign for the remainder of the year. After more
discussion, he accepted my decision and wished me well. My
discussion with Phyllis was similar, plus she added that Bogotá
had one of the most reputable eye clinics in the world, and if I did
come back, I could be assured of the very best care. If I had known
that earlier, I might have done things differently, and this story
would have a different ending. Apparently my doctors in the States
didn't know that, or hadn't thought it worthwhile to tell me, or just

dismissed the notion that a third-world country like Colombia could offer comparable treatment for my condition. Maybe my family had a part in influencing the doctors. Communication could be difficult between the two countries, and perhaps that played a role in the decision, as well. Whatever happened, I had let somebody else make the decision for me and didn't realize for a long time that there was no reason why I couldn't have had more of an input.

With that settled, my friends set out to help me enjoy the two weeks, and my schedule filled up quickly. Barb and I went shopping for *típicos* and found a beautiful leather bag and Christmas cards for next year decorated with prints of Colombian scenes. I bought a set of records called "Introduction to the Noble Song Book of Colombia" with a booklet which described in detail the history of Colombian music. Jerry and I went to Casa Vieja twice for *ajiaco*, and, as always, he was attentive if I needed anything. Paul, whom I hadn't heard from while I was in the States, came by one night with the box I had mailed to his shipping agent in Miami during Christmas. Several things were missing, and he said I could file an insurance claim if I wanted to, but it didn't seem worth the effort. Missing was a short red coat, six pewter cordial cups and two pairs of shorts, all of which could be replaced. Paul and I went out one more time, but I was right when I sensed earlier that our relationship would not be long lasting, even though he did show up in my life in the States again a few years later.

Nancy Ortiz had a tea for me after school at her house, and many teachers and administrators came. We took several pictures, and everybody looked happy in her beautiful home. One Saturday, Jerry, Movelle, Bruce, and I took a day trip to Zipaquirá, to the famous underground salt cathedral. It was impressive but I was thankful I didn't have to work in a salt mine. Another trip was to H. Stern, the famous jeweler, where we were ushered in and out under heavy guard. There was just no getting away from the firearms in Colombia. As I left the store, I turned my new emerald ring on my finger so the stone didn't show and the band looked like a wedding band. The clerks instructed us to do that since we were in *el centro*, where the crime rate was so high and where I'd had the incident with the red ruana and taxi several months earlier.

There was another trip to the school, a trip to Aviatur to finalize return reservations and as many nights out for dinner as we could work in, either in restaurants or somebody's house. The extra pounds I had gained earlier had miraculously dropped off while I was home, but I knew they would come back quickly if I didn't pay attention to how much I was eating, so I was conscious of the food.

The final trip was one I was afraid I would miss because of time, but fate was with me when I realized I could take a much longed for excursion down the Amazon. Jerry knew that I wanted to go and had found out details for a short trip. We would leave Saturday morning for the flight to Leticia, the southernmost town in Colombia, on the Amazon that also bordered Brazil and Peru. After a night in town, our plan was to hire a guide and boat for a Sunday and Monday tour of the river.

Our small jet landed at the nearly deserted airport around lunchtime, the first of two flights from Bogotá that came and went each day. We had heard that the drug cartels had moved into the sleepy area for easy access to the river and were building fine houses nearby. During the daytime drugs were often bought and sold on the streets, so we knew to be as inconspicuous and low key as possible. The local people were still trying to hold on to their agricultural and tourism interests, so we, and they, were prepared to arrange a fair deal for the river excursion.

Jerry and I headed to the hotel where we had reservations and, fortunately, had no problem securing our room. Traveling with our backpacks, we decided to keep them with us as we walked around the area. The sun was vicious, and already we noticed the mosquitoes, so having lotion and repellent close by was a necessity. At a café we sat in shade under a ceiling fan swatting flies while we ate sandwiches and drank beer. Drinking the water was out of the question. It felt like a scene from the movie *Casablanca* with the cool tile floors and verdant foliage and oppressive heat stirred only by the languid fan.

We stirred up our own energy soon and found the store that handled the river tours, to plan for our outing. We decided on a two-day, one-night plan that would include everything for one price, and then returned to the hotel for a siesta. The hotel was clean and sparse and adequate. We shared a room with two single beds, a private bath, and were happy to have a comfortable, and we hoped, safe place to stay. After a good nap we were up and out again but found no place to go except the one restaurant where we again ate a typical Colombian meal, meat, rice, potatoes, plantains, and salad. When we finished, there was nothing to do but return to the hotel. We sat on the verandah and sipped gin and tonic, and then turned in. The jungle sounds were again close by and I thought about the creatures out there. We each had brought a small book to read, but I doubt if either of us read more than ten minutes before falling into a deep sleep. Jerry and I had become such close friends that we had no qualms about sharing a room. I felt safe with him and we understood each other. This time I dreamed of falling through space with a blood- pressure cuff unwrapping from my head as I tumbled through the darkness.

We rose early the next morning and showered and dressed quickly. Before dressing, I covered my skin in suntan lotion and insect repellant and then put on full-length jeans, a long-sleeved white cotton blouse, sneakers with socks, and a full-brim hat. I couldn't imagine that I would not be suffering from the heat in all of those clothes, but people told us we HAD to cover up and we would be okay once on the river. We had a quick breakfast and then walked to the dock.

Our guide was a young man who seemed bored with us, but appeared to know what he was doing, so we jumped in the boat. Jerry sat in the front, I was in the middle, and the guide was in the back. I didn't know much about boats, but this one was wooden, about 15 feet long with a 35-horsepower motor. For an hour we just rode and looked at the banks. The river reminded me at that point, of Lake Waccamaw in Columbus County, where I spent many happy, childhood days. It was swampy, dark, rather mysterious looking, and I knew I didn't want to water ski in it.

We soon pulled over to the bank where some children almost magically appeared to help us tie up the boat, and we got out to stretch our legs and look around. Pedro, the guide, finally started talking to us, but I could understand very little of what he was saying. Even Jerry, who had a much better command of Spanish than I did, said he didn't recognize the guide's dialect at all, but could understand enough to communicate. The children were interested in my camera, and after taking a few pictures and finishing up a roll of film, I unwrapped a new one and gave the film wrapper to them when they stretched out their hands. I don't know why they wanted the paper but they took it, examined it carefully and smiled. We then walked to a little village and looked at the houses of the people who lived there. Built on stilts on the edge of the water, they were basically a floor and a roof attached with ropes. In a clearing was a communal cooking area where several women, topless and wearing red sarongs around their hips, and their children were sitting. They were all very shy and avoided eye contact with us. Through the guide, they offered us some fruit, and we took it gratefully. They also showed us some paintings done on bark, which were bright and colorful and depicted jungle themes: snakes, monkeys, and crocodiles. I bought a couple and left a few extra pesos with them. The few men looked at us and smiled as we smiled back. That was about all we could share with these gentle people. Soon it was time to leave, so Jerry and I each found a clump of bushes to hide behind to use the bathroom, and I figured out that's what our bathroom facilities would be like for this entire excursion.

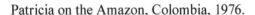

Patricia on the Amazon, Colombia, 1976.

Back on the river the banks were getting farther apart and the sun was getting higher as we headed to our next stop. The breeze was very refreshing, and I was surprised that the heat wasn't more uncomfortable. We soon pulled over again, splashed through the edge of the water, and walked to a little shed where Pedro told us we would have lunch. We had already eaten our fruit, and it was delicious, but we were hungry for more. I never found out its name, but it was similar to a mango and quenched our thirst in a hurry. For lunch, we had *sancocho*, a wonderful hot potato soup, which seemed like a strange choice for a midday meal on the Amazon, but which was actually very satisfying and filling. With the soup we drank coke. After lunch we saw a wild boar walking around the shed, which Jerry actually approached while I snapped a picture. Pedro pointed out some huge water lilies at the water's edge and also an old man paddling his homemade canoe down the river. I kept my eyes open for an anaconda and was relieved when I didn't see one in the undergrowth as we walked back to the boat.

After about an hour on the water, we approached another village, just across the border into Peru, where the Yagua Indian tribe lived. They looked very much like the other Indians but were smaller. They all, the men and women alike, wore grass skirts, and that was all. A few of the men wore paint, or berry stains, on their faces, and they all had beautiful nut-brown skin and straight black hair. They were selling their handicrafts as well and offered jewelry, more paintings, masks, and utensils used in cooking. I bought a mask and two necklaces, which were made from different nuts and berries, which I put around my neck immediately. We paid a fair price for our purchases and took a few more pictures. Impressed by the kindness and gentleness of these Amazon people, I was aware that I might never see them again and was grateful for this opportunity and a few moments of reflection. I looked at them carefully and imbedded their images in my mind. Soon, we were on our way again and headed to the unknown place where we would spend the night.

As we rode down the river late in the afternoon and absorbed the rays from the setting sun, we marveled at the remote villages we had just visited and tried to assimilate the day. This was one of those events that probably wouldn't happen many times in our lives, if ever again, and we were humbled by the experience. We had witnessed a primitive culture that was unknown to many people in the world. Would they survive? What would happen to them in the next fifty years? Would they still be selling their trinkets to the few tourists who came through? Or would they head to the towns and cities to explore a new world? We felt as if we were experiencing an achievement of our own when we walked through their villages and acknowledged these people and the value of their lives.

As we approached our lodgings, still on the river, we thought about a glass of wine or beer before having our dinner. Jerry mentioned it to the guide and asked if something would be available when we arrived. No, he indicated, but he would stop somewhere and get a bottle of wine for us. A few minutes later he pulled over again, tied up the boat to a tree trunk and walked to a nearby house. It was on stilts, at the water's edge, just like all the houses we had seen, and was Carolina blue. It put a smile on my face. He was back quickly with a bottle of wine that had a Chilean label, and we were looking forward to getting settled somewhere and enjoying it. Before we pulled away in the boat, it occurred to me that we didn't have a corkscrew. How could we open it? What happened next will stay in my mind forever, I'm sure, and I've never seen it happen since. Pedro took the bottle to the banks of the river, where the soil was damp but firm, squatted down, and with a mighty thrust downward, slammed the base of the bottle into the earth. A few more stabs and the cork miraculously popped out. We were amazed and fortunately, I was holding my camera and managed to get a picture just in case no one believed me later. He picked up the cork, reinserted it, hopped back in the boat and off we went again. Jerry held the bottle as if it were a baby needing protection, and we were laughing and patting Pedro on his shoulder with congratulations for accomplishing this magnificent feat. We were happy, sunburned, dirty and thirsty.

Not long after that, Pedro guided the boat to a small, protected cove where we saw our lodgings for the night. It was a pontoon boat, moored at the edge of the water, with a screened-in area where there were six cots, stacked three deep. There was a hammock, a stool, a small resident monkey, and an outhouse at the end of the boat, which emptied into the water. There was even a roll of toilet paper, which was a nice amenity, but I still had plenty in my backpack. At last, a place to sit down!

Pedro gave us our itinerary for the rest of the night as we moved from one boat to another. He was staying in a house nearby but would bring us our dinner eventually. It would rain around 9 p.m., he said, and when that was over, he would come back and take us on the crocodile hunt. After breakfast the next morning, we'd travel back to Leticia where we could shower before catching the late afternoon flight into Bogotá.

As soon as he left, we settled down with the wine and some crackers I had in my bag. There was still plenty of sunlight, and after a while we started talking about taking a dip in the river. We were hot, covered in suntan lotion and insect repellent. With no shower facilities on board, a quick swim sounded tempting. We really weren't concerned about piranhas or snakes or other creatures and quickly decided to jump in. Shedding our clothes, except for my underwear, we eased over the side of the boat and fell in the water. It was cool and refreshing and felt heavenly. We splashed around a while and eventually caught sight of Pedro, fishing, nearby. We reasoned that if we had seen him, he probably would have seen us, and decided to get back on board and put some clothes on, which we did. However, before that happened, we grabbed the camera and took a few pictures of each other. We felt rejuvenated, so our mission was accomplished.

It wasn't long before we saw Pedro walking down the little hill from the house, carrying a basket with what we thought would be our dinner. His earlier fishing excursion had yielded some fresh fish and that was the main course. I didn't recognize the fish, but it was fried, and was served with platanos, also fried, and rice and bananas. He also brought us a liter bottle of fresh water. Jerry sat on the stool and insisted I sit in the hammock for our evening meal, and we settled down to experience our food as if we were in a fine restaurant. It turned out to be delectable. By now it was dark and we ate slowly, talked long and finished the wine.

My relationship with Jerry had always been one of friendship. He was like a well-loved and respected brother, although I probably would not have gone skinny-dipping with a brother. There were other men in my life who held my romantic interests, and I just didn't think of Jerry that way. He never sent out signals that he wanted to take our relationship to another level, but I sensed that he would have been willing had I made the first move. To do so on my part would have been purely selfish and I didn't want to risk losing a highly valued friendship. But I'll admit I was tempted that night and, years later, often wondered what held me back from a man who was so devoted and kind.

By the time the rain started we were stretched out on the deck and mellow and succumbed to the gentle movement of the water for a quiet and peaceful rest before the hunt.

At 10:00 pm sharp, Pedro appeared and led us to his boat. The rain had stopped, the air was cool and the nighttime sounds from the jungle had changed. The boat eased into the water slowly, and we listened and watched carefully as Pedro quietly pointed out lights on the surface of the water, which were the eyes of crocodiles. He wore a miner's hat, with a flashlight on the front, and we followed the light as much as we could. I could almost touch the night, and it nearly took my breath away. The symphony being played around us was almost overwhelming, and I sensed we were in a place where human beings didn't belong.

I was really not anxious to spear a crocodile and would have been satisfied to just ride in the boat, but, after more exploring and sliding through the dark water, Pedro speared a small one, tied it to the boat and we soon headed back. Jerry and I were both quiet and somewhat stunned when we saw that, and as soon as we got back to the pontoon, we asked Pedro to let the crocodile go. It was still thrashing about in the water, and I couldn't imagine that anybody would want to keep such a helpless creature. Did the guides think that most tourists wanted and expected a crocodile hunt? Did they? I never had a desire to capture a crocodile and felt a little guilty for having just taken part in that activity that was nothing more than a self-indulgent sport. If I ever came back, I vowed not to schedule any kind of hunt ever again.

The experience of being on the Amazon, however, at that time of night, surrounded by the jungle, witnessing this part of the world, from this particular vantage point, moved me greatly and humbled me. I didn't sleep much that night but tossed and turned with thoughts of everything from the Amazon-monkeys, piranhas, dugout canoes, masks, Indians, grass skirts, and mosquitoes. When morning finally came, we were ready to return to Bogotá.

We arrived back at our apartment before dark, and since Jerry had taken a day off from school to go on the trip, he was anxious to get back to his place and catch up on some school work. My most pressing need was to take a long shower and then start getting things together for the trip back to the States. My household goods would be shipped out with the other teachers' things in June, but they had to be packed and everything itemized before I left in a couple of days. If there was anything else to go, friends had offered to take it with them when they returned. Dot was planning a trip to the States during the summer to introduce Lucía to her family and hoped to come to North Carolina. She offered to bring any remaining items, but I left most of the household things we had been sharing. She would be staying in Colombia at least one more year and would need the kitchen things, especially. Other friends called the next day, and we said goodbye again.

On the night before I left, Terry, my principal, invited Dot and me and Jerry to his house for dinner. It was a small group, and we enjoyed a wonderful meal with him and his wife. They were gracious and supportive and offered, one more time, to help in any way they could. I had decided to go to the airport alone on departure day since so many people from the school had taken time away from work while I was there, and I was beginning to feel guilty about all the attention. We parted on a solid note that night as we left Terry's house, and I was full of gratitude for all they had done. It was time to go home—to the U.S.

For the rest of my life, Colombia would be a unique and cherished part of my past. I truly thought I would never return and relied on memories and the letters I wrote to my parents, which they saved, to remind me that I had followed through on the pursuit of a dream. I had lived and worked in a foreign culture, improved my Spanish skills and maybe contributed in a small way to improving relations between two countries with a fractious history. I had witnessed different life styles, marveled at the physical beauty of a new country, and met some people I would hold close to my heart and never forget. I found out that all children, regardless of their backgrounds, respond to love and support and a kind word. I also acknowledged my debt and gratitude to CNG. This had been the ultimate adventure for me.

My souvenirs were my memories of CNG, the wind and rain, my red ruana, *el centro*, DAS, *ajiaco*, the Witches Conference, the Gold Museum, our apartment at calle 52-A con 27-A, security meetings, Melgar, bicycle races, Omar Sharif, coffee, the Amazon, and aguardiente. If I had to identify one memory that stands out among them all, it would be the memory of friends, some of whom miraculously showed up in my life again. They were the glue that held the experience together and gave it value.

Fate has a way of intervening when we least expect it, and, I soon found out, that I was not through with Colombia yet. Old and new friends would appear and enrich my life, a new Colombian school and city would take their place on my resumé, and my own family would expand. The ultimate adventure would resume, and I'd be given another chance to continue the journey.

Transition

Six years passed before I saw Colombia again, and when I did it was the city of Cali, self-proclaimed Salsa capital of the world, sports city of Colombia, and "branch of heaven."

In the intervening years, I had married, divorced, and had grown up a lot. Eventually, I returned to New Bern and the Craven County Schools and found a different life than I had known when I first left eight years earlier. Most of my single friends were now married and starting families, several of my married friends were divorced or remarried, and I was faced with the prospect of carving out a new life. My job teaching math was always important, and I spent a lot of time on work. I stayed busy with activities, civic and social, and new people I met through work. But I missed the cohesiveness of our group in Bogotá and people who shared my passion for travel and foreign cultures. My closest friend and traveling companion, Marilyn, and I took a three week-trip to London one summer, but she and her husband, Sam, lived four hours away in Myrtle Beach, and I didn't see them often. I visited Mexico with relatives. When opportunities to travel arose, I always took advantage of them and kept my eyes open for new adventures. But truthfully, I often felt out of place and unsettled.

Two of my dad's brothers and their wives had traveled with the Friendship Force of North Carolina to England and on a later trip, to Scotland. They stayed with families on these cultural exchanges and raved about their experiences. When I saw an article about a new exchange for the summer of 1982 with Dubrovnik, I was definitely interested. One of my aunts told me she was applying for the same trip. Soon, we were both on the list to a place neither of us had visited. Just the kind of summer experience I was looking for.

We filled out forms with personal information, such as favorite foods, hobbies, previous travel experiences and sent a current picture. Apparently, the Friendship Force would try to place us with a family that shared the same interests, but they couldn't promise that. The only guarantee was a cultural immersion that could open doors to understanding through the power of friendship, regardless of cultural differences. I felt connected immediately.

Two weeks before our departure, we received notice that Dubrovnik had been cancelled and a new city had been chosen. The planners would announce the name of the city soon. If anyone preferred not to take part in the exchange, they could apply for and receive a refund. A bit let down, but curious at the same time, I kept an open mind.

When Cali, Colombia, was announced as the new destination, I was stunned. Hugely disappointed, I seriously considered canceling the trip. It wasn't that I didn't want to visit Colombia again: more than that, with my limited resources for traveling, I wanted to experience a new country. My aunt, however, was thrilled about the choice and looked forward to visiting a country she had never seen before, so I felt obligated to honor my commitment. And what an honor it turned out to be. Cali was so different from Bogotá that, in the end, I felt like I *had* been to a new country.

¡Bienvenido!

On July 1, 1982, after a chartered Friendship Force flight from the Raleigh-Durham airport and a turbulent final thirty minutes that had most of us clinging to our armrests, we slammed into the tarmac and waited for the plane to explode. Fortunately, that didn't happen, but a lot of screaming took place before we caught our breath and realized we were safe. I knew our Colombian crew was well trained in flying around the Andes, but I still grimaced when the wheels screeched and we bounced against each other. I had almost forgotten what these flights were sometimes like and instinctively crossed myself.

As we deplaned and walked across the tarmac, I noticed the warm, sunny day and immediately started making comparisons to Bogotá. I had never seen Bogotá in this clear, bright light, and not until we walked inside the terminal did I sense anything familiar. The aromas of empanadas, pineapples and coffee brought back a wealth of memories. Even though warm outside and not a ruana in sight, I managed to conjure a scent of wet wool. As we passed easily through Customs and Immigration, I heard again the Spanish of Colombia, but it had a softer edge than what I remembered from the higher altitude in Bogotá. Employees smiled and projected a sense of welcome I hadn't experienced before in this country.

The armed guards, however, seemed to have multiplied, and their firearms were as imposing as ever. I had kept up with the political situation in Colombia and knew that there were still kidnappings, violence, and terrorism which, at times, were intense.

The drug lords were controlling much of the economy, and many people continued to live in fear. FARC (Revolutionary Armed Forces of Colombia) remained a threat and was still a militant, leftist group, but reports indicated that the Revolution was declining into simple, money-driven hooliganism. According to what I read, most guerillas couldn't even read, much less understand anything about Marx, and the conflicts all seemed to be about money. So that aspect of life in Colombia hadn't changed.

When I walked outside to meet my new family, no fear of terrorism was obvious. Other than the guards in military uniforms juggling their rifles and looking at the American Friendship Force with curiosity, the airport could have been anywhere in the States. People were milling about, smiling, their sleek black hair shining in the sun, contrasting with the white shirts and blouses that nearly all of them wore. Almost everyone was waving a placard with someone's name. The Colombians had the names of their guests, but we didn't know the names of our assigned families. After my Aunt Frances and I had gone through Customs together, and as we looked for our names, she said, "You are my *sobrina* (niece), right? I want to tell my family you're here, too." Aunt Frances had learned a few words in Spanish before leaving and was looking forward to trying them out.

"Yes, and you're my *tía* (aunt). Have a great time if I don't see you again." We didn't know if we would cross paths in the next ten days but knew we could make contact in any emergency.

Almost immediately, I spotted a short, friendly-looking man holding a colorful poster with the name "Patricia." When I walked over to greet him, he gallantly picked up my suitcase. His name was Eduardo, and he introduced his young daughter Anna, who was grinning and giddy with excitement. His wife, Mercedes, he told me, was waiting for us at their apartment. Anna and I got in the backseat of the car and waited for him to put the suitcase in the small trunk. His car had no air conditioning, so all the windows were rolled down. As we left the airport and took advantage of the warm breeze flowing through the car, I secretly praised my decision to have an Afro-style permanent before leaving. Not knowing what to expect in terms of bathroom facilities, I thought that would be the easiest hairdo – just wash and pick. Now I was sure I had done the right thing.

The ten-mile trip into Cali, the third largest city in Colombia, was through a sleepy countryside where farm animals grazed and coffee and sugarcane fields dotted the landscape. At 3,271 ft, the city is located in the Cauca Valley in western Colombia and once had an economy based on livestock, sugarcane, fruit and panela (a sugar derivative). In the 19th century, Cali was a quiet community of 20,000 people surrounded by mango plantations and communal lands, transferred from the Spanish Crown to the impoverished classes. Around 1890 a private company built the market plaza, which it later sold to the Cali municipality in 1921. The plaza was still an important place today in this city of over two million people. The coffee and sugar industries brought prosperity to the sleepy little mountain town.

Completely bordered by mountains, the city is mainly flat, but areas in the western part are mountainous. That mountain range screens the flow of humidity from the Pacific coast and accounts for the semi-tropical climate. With an average temperature of 74 degrees Fahrenheit and fresh afternoon breezes, Cali enjoys a temperate climate all year. Near the Equator, there are no major seasonal variations. Rain can fall at any time, nourishing the lush green countryside. Pretty close to perfect, I thought.

Eduardo maneuvered the car into the city traffic and soon pulled up in front of a five-story building. Parking the small Renault on the narrow sidewalk, he told Anna and me to get out and that he would meet us upstairs.

My Spanish was rusty, but, so far, I had understood most of what Eduardo said, especially when he spoke slowly. Understanding seven-year-old Anna, however, was another story. Still excited and full of girlish giggles, she thought if she spoke loudly and slowly enough, I would understand her. I nodded my head and smiled. As we walked up the stairs to the third floor, she wanted to carry my pocketbook and hold my hand, so that's how we arrived at the apartment. Mercedes, her mother, was standing at the open door.

"Welcome, Patricia. Our house is your house. Please come in," she said in Spanish.

"Thank you," I replied, "I'm very happy to meet you," as we clasped hands. Not in the Bogotá fashion of clasping wrists, but actually clasping hands.

My first view of the apartment was a room with a dentist's chair placed right in the middle. Noting my surprise, she quickly said, "I'm a dentist and this is where I see my patients." She waved her arm around the room and seemed very proud of the space. Diplomas were prominently displayed on the walls.

She and Anna then showed me around the apartment: the kitchen and maid's quarters, dining room, living room, their bedrooms, the bathroom and then my bedroom. All the floors were tile, and healthy lush plants were in every room. By that time Eduardo had come in and put my suitcase in my room.

"We'll have lunch in about thirty minutes, so make yourself at home," Mercedes said. "After that, you can rest."

The four of us sat down to bowls of steaming broth, with vegetables and cilantro swimming on top. As my taste buds suddenly erupted, I realized I hadn't experienced that exquisite flavor in six years. This was followed by a piece of beef, seared in a frying pan with garlic, salt and pepper and a seasoning I couldn't identify. On the side was a whopping serving of rice with onions. Next came a crisp green salad with tomatoes, cucumber, and more cilantro, topped with a simple dressing of oil and vinegar. We washed all of this down with *jugo de lulo,* a juice made with the lulo fruit. I had never found a comparable fruit, but it was light in color, thick in texture, and needed a lot of sugar. It was tasty and filling.

The entire family ate with gusto and, of course, so did I. I noticed the Colombian custom, which I had seen in Bogotá, of resting one's elbows or forearms on the table. What an adjustment it had been for me to try to stop doing that when I returned to the States. After a while I didn't even try. This wonderful custom, I thought, illustrated one's engagement with the people sharing your meal. So, I thought of elbows on the table as a compliment to those sharing your food. When the meal was finally over, I was stuffed, and grateful that most Colombians ate their big meal during the day and very little at night.

After the overnight flight and no sleep, I was ready to shower and lie down. The host families all knew we'd be tired on that first day, so Mercedes indicated I could go to my room and rest as long as I needed.

It wasn't long before I was clean and comfortably ensconced in my bedroom, thinking about the upcoming ten days and what Cali had in store. I quickly fell into a deep sleep.

I awoke a few hours later to the sound of men's voices but couldn't understand what they were saying. Occasionally I heard Mercedes' voice, but, again, couldn't translate. I took my time getting ready because I didn't want to interrupt whatever was going on, perhaps a dental appointment. Eventually, however, I left my room and walked to the room where four people were sitting and talking.

"Ah, Patricia," one of the men said as I walked in the room. "We're with the Friendship Force, and we're afraid a terrible mistake has been made. Eduardo, was actually waiting for another lady whose name is also Patricia." At this point I asked if he could speak in English since I was losing track of what he was saying. "Of course," he replied in English. "We need you to get your things and come with us. We'll take you to the family that is waiting for you. They are very worried."

I looked inquisitively at Mercedes and she nodded. "Yes, you need to go with them," she said.

I quickly returned to my room and repacked. I said goodbye to Mercedes and Anna, who had just come in the room, near tears. I thanked them for their hospitality and asked them to thank Eduardo. As we left the apartment quickly, I had the feeling that somebody was in trouble.

On the way to my new home, the men told me a little about the family I was getting ready to meet. They were Marta and Esteban Plata, a young couple in their twenties with no children, married for about a year. Esteban owned and operated Northside Pizzeria and was planning to expand his business by opening another pizzeria soon. Marta helped out at times. Both were from families that had lived in Cali for several generations, and both had many relatives in the area. Esteban's sister and her husband, Ximena and Rafael Franco, were hosting a couple from Raleigh. One of the men knew the Plata family personally and said, "I think there are nine siblings, and most are married with children of their own. It's a big family. *Muy grande,"* he said and smiled. "You'll enjoy them."

We left the city streets and drove through a residential area. Before we arrived at the Platas' apartment, it flashed through my mind that these strangers could be taking me anywhere. This was probably how people were kidnapped, and, at that moment, I was truly at the mercy of their good intentions. As soon as I thought that I realized there wasn't a lot I could do and tried to concentrate on the next step. The ride felt very cloak and dagger.

When we pulled into an underground garage, the driver spoke to the portero, who called the apartment. My escorts expertly ushered me to the elevator and then to the second floor where the door to the apartment suddenly flung open. There stood a small, lovely young woman who clasped her hands in what seemed like great relief.

"Ah, Patricia, we have been so worried about you. I am Marta, and Esteban will be here soon. Please come in." As we clasped hands, I immediately felt her genuine concern. She was speaking in Spanish, and I couldn't understand everything, but I immediately understood that she was happy that I had finally arrived. The Friendship Force people explained to her what had happened at the airport and soon left.

"Patricia, please sit down. Would you like something to drink? Some juice?" Marta asked.

"Juice would be fine," I answered.

While she was in the kitchen, I looked around the living room and admired the modern furnishings, sleek leather sofa and matching chairs, graphic framed prints on the wall, an organ, shiny tile floors, and an abundance of healthy, verdant plants. There were also a few family pictures on a small table. It was dark outside now, and the curtains were pulled, but I could see sliding glass doors.

When Marta returned with the juice, she asked about the flight and then told me about what had happened at the airport. She and Esteban had gone to the airport to meet me with the picture I had sent in the original application. And then it dawned on me what had happened. The picture I sent was taken a few months before the trip, and before I decided to cut and perm my hair. They were looking for a person with long blond hair, not a short, curly 'fro. As people were picked up by their host families, they gradually realized I wasn't there. By that time, I was probably in the car with Eduardo and Anna, headed into town. Marta and Esteban contacted officials, questions were tossed all around and even the Police Department was involved.

Kidnappings were a way of life in Colombia, and the idea that an American woman traveling with the Friendship Force might be kidnapped was not unusual. It would have been a significant way for some group to make a statement, and the Colombian Friendship Force organization was terrified that that might have happened.

While all of this was going on, the other Patricia was at the airport, waiting, with no idea where her family was. Finally, someone made the connection between our names and sent the three men out to Eduardo and Mercedes' house to look for me. Gratefully, no kidnapping occurred, and I was horrified that so much time had been spent sorting out the mix up. We were probably all at fault, but I feel sure that that kind of mix up probably never happened again with the Friendship Force in Cali.

I realized pretty quickly that my Spanish was more than a little rusty and that communicating would be a challenge. Marta spoke little English, but somehow, we managed to express our ideas. When she showed me my room, I understood where I could put my clothes, how to work the light switch and, when I needed clothes washed, where to put them for the maid who came during the day. Marta showed me the bathroom just for me. She also pointed out the towels, and I noticed there was a washcloth, which was something Colombians, like Europeans, didn't use. So she had provided that just for me. I noticed there were electrical outlets for my hair dryer and the contact lens case I used to clean my lenses daily.

While I was unpacking, Esteban called on the phone and Marta told him I had finally arrived. She then told me we were going out as soon as he returned. I asked her if what I was wearing, a skirt, t-shirt, and sandals, was appropriate. She looked at me carefully and said "Fine, but you need to take a sweater." It was July and I couldn't imagine needing a sweater, but I pulled one from my suitcase.

We went back to the living room to wait for Esteban, and soon he was knocking on the door. "Hola, Hola, anybody home?" Marta hopped up and went to open the door. A quick peck on the cheek for her and he was in the room. He was the first Colombian man I had ever seen who was tall and, not only was he tall, but he was also handsome. The Colombian women were famous for their beauty, but the men were not. It never seemed to bother the men I had known, but seeing a tall, healthy, handsome young man was a surprise. The first thing he said to me was, "Ah, la secuestrada" (the kidnapped woman). He was friendly, welcoming, and when he realized that I wasn't fluent in Spanish, said, "No importa" (it doesn't matter). And that was the way we dealt with the language barrier for the next ten days. It just didn't matter.

For a short while the three of us sat in the living room and talked as much as we could. Then, Esteban said, "Let's go to the pizzeria!"

After a short ride to the restaurant, which was located on *Avenida Sexta,* (sixth avenue), we walked into an outdoor dining area with tables for four or six people. It was early evening, music was playing, and people seemed to be having a good time. The warm afternoon had changed into a fresh, temperate night, cooled by the afternoon breezes that swept through the valley. Candles flickered on all the tables. Esteban guided us to a long table, and I sat down among people I didn't know and could barely talk to. Marta was on my left and Esteban was up being the host. As everybody welcomed me, I felt completely at ease.

"Would you like a beer, Patricia?" someone asked. Before I could even answer, a tall, full glass was placed in front of me.

Everyone called me by name as if they had known me for a long time. The woman to my right said, "Patricia, are you tired? I know it's been a long day for you," in English. "I'm Ximena, Esteban's sister, and this is my husband, Rafael." He also spoke in English but quickly said, "We're practicing our English." I thought they were doing fine with their English and we continued talking.

"Do you know Mary and Vernon from Raleigh? They are staying with us," Ximena said. I looked across the table at the American couple whom I had not seen on the plane. We acknowledged each other and continued with our attempts to communicate within the group.

Salads soon arrived, followed quickly by several pizzas placed on the table. It was a noisy group with laughter and high spirits floating along the sounds of Colombian music. Marta told me that most of the twelve or fourteen people there were family members, and I wondered what it would be like to have so many brothers and sisters. Or to be an in-law in a family that large.

Before we left the pizzeria, Ximena mentioned that we were going to the river the next day and that she and Rafael would be bringing their two daughters. I was thrilled about that because I remembered well the days on the river with friends in the Bogotá area. She made a special effort to be helpful and make me comfortable, and I appreciated it.

When we arrived back at the apartment, Marta and Esteban, both solicitous, wanted to be sure I had everything I needed. I did. We made a few plans for the river trip, and then we all turned in.

The next morning the three of us and Xavier, one of Esteban's brothers, packed the car with food and supplies and headed South to the National Park, *Farallones de Cali*. Xavier had been at the pizzeria the night before, but I didn't remember him. Just as handsome as Esteban, he was the only brother at that time who was single. The Park was about an hour's drive south, and by the time we reached the parking area we were in the mountains. Several cars were already there, and I soon saw Ximena, Rafael, and their two adorable young daughters, Maria Isabel, eight, and Margarita, five. I spoke to Mary and Vernon Penny from Raleigh and recognized other people from the night before. There were a *lot* of children with the group today, and I could tell by comments from their parents, they had all been coached on minding their manners. They talked to me and the Pennys, walked beside us, held our hands when we crossed brooks or rough terrain and made themselves indispensable. They were all delightful.

The whole group walked a couple of miles on a trail through the Park, to a secluded spot where we set up camp for the day. Marta, Ximena, and some of the other women started preparing food, while the men built a fire in a stone pit. They also set up a small tent for the children, who were happily scampering around.

The Pennys and I offered to help, but everybody insisted that we rest or just look around. The women were slicing vegetables, shucking corn, smashing garlic, and rinsing chicken with water they had brought with them. They pulled out pots and pans and started stirring things together. When Xavier and others offered to show us around the park, we took them up on it.

The first thing we saw was a waterfall that snaked down the side of the mountain and spilled into a pool that seemed to beckon.

"After lunch," Xavier said, grinning, as if reading our minds, "we'll go swimming."

We walked slowly as views of the mountains became more expansive. I still had lingering feelings of nostalgia for this country, and I was overcome with emotion as I took in the majesty of the panorama. What was the hold Colombia had on me? I didn't know but couldn't deny that my feelings were strong. We soon approached two men and a young boy who were loading bags of coffee beans and bananas on the back of a donkey. One of the men, in red polyester pants, had a pompadour hairdo with sideburns. He stood erect, with pride, as he tied the cargo to the donkey. The young boy moved with a lightning-quick energy and wore a short ruana to ward off the chill of the mountains. Xavier spoke to them for a couple of minutes and we moved on.

Along the way I took pictures, smelled the flowers, walked clear of a bull grazing nearby, and before long we were back on the path to the camp. We could smell the savory aroma of our lunch before we arrived, and familiar pangs of hunger hit all of us at the same time.

"*Huele delicioso,*" Xavier said, smiling. Yes, indeed, it does smell delicious, I thought. As soon as we were in view of the campsite, I noticed that Esteban was filming all of us with a movie camera. I had noticed some very nice camera equipment in the apartment and thought that must be his hobby.

After a quick trip to an outhouse, we washed our hands with water they had brought, and got in line for bowls of the soup, called *Sancocho*. It was similar to *Ajiaco but* was not served with the condiments. Full of chicken, corn, onions and different types of potatoes, it was slightly thick and seasoned with cilantro, garlic, and a lot of pepper. It could not have tasted any better. We sat on the ground under shade trees and ate quietly until everybody had their fill and then went back for more. Even the children were engrossed in this magnificent production.

After the wonderful meal, everybody rested, and no one even attempted to clean up. When the siestas were over, we walked to the swimming area and took a refreshing dip under the waterfall we saw earlier. The siesta and swim rejuvenated all of us, and we soon packed everything in the cars and returned to Cali.

Our host families honored us that day by preparing this typical dish in a typical cultural setting and sharing it with us. I was grateful. It was an all-day affair with a lot of people involved, and I acknowledged with amazement how gracefully they had carried it off.

Before going to bed that night, Marta and Esteban said we would go to *Piedechinche,* a restored sugarcane plantation, the next day. I fell asleep and dreamed of swimming in a chlorinated pool full of cilantro.

During the 18th and 19th centuries, the sugarcane industry thrived in the fertile Cauca Valley. Sugar barons built haciendas, and small communities developed around these plantations. Several of the haciendas survived into the twentieth century, and a few had been restored and were open as museums.

Xavier arrived at the apartment early and rode with us to *Piedechinche*, one of the best-preserved haciendas. Ximena and her family met us there along with Esteban and Ximena's mother, Nora, and their aunt, Cila, who lived with Nora. Nora had been a widow for many years and had raised her nine children as a single parent. Cila had no children and was a valued member of the family. They all welcomed me as if I were a long-lost relative.

The museum was full of tools and instruments used for the cultivation of the sugarcane plant. Domestic objects, such as cast-iron pots, irons, and delicate linens were also on display and looked just like the ones from the same era I had seen in Tryon Palace in New Bern. Documents recorded the history of the growth of the sugar industry. Furniture stuffed with horsehair or covered in leather was hand-made on the plantation. A few pieces were of European origin and spoke to the fact that the people who lived there were well-traveled. Oil portraits on the walls and old photographs showed men, women, and children dressed in the same styles I had seen my own ancestors wear in family pictures. People here in Colombia seemed to have lived just as my family had lived many years ago. In the nearby stable, several spotless and gleaming carriages were lined up as if waiting for their horses. Bridles, tackle, and saddles hung on the walls and looked very familiar.

The restored grounds and gardens reflected a balance among plants, insects, and birds. The trees and shrubbery were brought from diverse regions of Colombia where the sugarcane culture flourished. I had never seen such huge leaves on so many different plants and marveled at the variety. Nora and Cila admired the orchids and called me over to take a sniff, which was heavenly.

As Esteban and Xavier continued filming, we relaxed in a cabana while waiting for our late-day meal. The afternoon stretched out languorously.

On Monday morning Esteban and Xavier took me and the Pennys to a bank to exchange traveler's checks for pesos. So far, we hadn't needed pesos, but we wanted to shop before leaving and knew we needed a few. Esteban was interested in buying dollars, and I was able to sell him forty dollars in cash. I remembered that most Colombians were happy to get U.S. dollars for future trips abroad. After more sightseeing they dropped me off at the apartment and took the Pennys back to Ximena's house. Unsure about what to wear to an upcoming event the following night, I asked Marta to help me choose something appropriate to wear. She picked out the more conservative of two dresses I had brought with me, a dark purple, long-sleeved, knee-length dress.

The Friendship Force organization had planned a reception for all the FF participants and their host families in honor of our July 4th Independence Day celebration. At the impressive and formal gathering, Colombian and Stateside representatives gave short speeches before dinner. Unfortunately, one of the Friendship Force advisors from the States discovered *aguardiente* and was barely able to stand up, much less give a speech. The only redeeming factor was that, because of the language barrier, his sloppy faux pas may not have been obvious to the Colombians. When that embarrassing episode was over, recordings of the two National Anthems were played, and I was once again enthralled by the majesty and beauty of the Colombian anthem. The steak dinner for three hundred people proceeded smoothly. As far as I could tell, Xavier and Esteban took turns filming.

Our host families got a break the next day when the US FF took an optional bus trip to Sylvia, a small mountain village about two hours away. This was the day the Indians in the area came to the market to display and sell their goods. After a restful ride up the mountain, people on the bus started putting on jackets and sweaters. I had packed my short, lightweight ruana from Bogotá and quickly remembered how perfect it was for the mountains.

As we approached the town, I noticed how tiny the people were and their beautiful clothes. The men and women both wore bowler hats and ruanas. The women wore black, mid-length skirts with a few rows of bright pink trim. Their short ruanas were purple with the same pink trim. They wore black lace-up shoes and black socks. Around their necks were white, cowl-neck collars. Some of them wore a strap around their shoulders which held down the ruana and tied in the back. The men showed more variety in their ruanas. They were gray, brown, or brown and white plaid. They wore skirts similar to the women's, but without the pink trim. The shoes were the same that the women wore. The children wore variations on these styles with caps instead of hats.

As we walked among them, I became aware of how gentle and shy they were. Avoiding eye contact, they smiled and looked away. The vendors in the market, however, were more vocal, and didn't hesitate to speak to us in their unique dialect. I tried to communicate but failed to say much more than "How much?" and "How beautiful." I bought a hand-knitted child's cap with long, side straps, typical of the local style.

The area of the market where food was displayed was rumbling with activity. Since we were not buying food, we simply watched and listened. I decided to take a picture of a woman who was selling fruit and baskets, and when I pulled out my camera, she threw up her hand in my direction, and shouted "NO!" I quickly put my camera back in my purse. In the main plaza huge oak trees provided plenty of shade. The sun was bright, the temperature cool, and we found a comfortable spot to sit while eating our bag lunches, which we had brought from Cali. After more sightseeing we climbed back on the bus for the return trip to Cali. Our guide pointed out the tranquil river that skirted around the town and was the lifeline for the community.

Esteban picked me up at the bus stop and wanted to know everything about the trip: what I ate, what I bought, and what I thought of the Indians. He really seemed to care, and I gave my Spanish a good workout. When we got back to the apartment, he and Marta told me about our upcoming trip to Lake Calima. It would be an overnight trip, and we'd swim, go boating, and waterski. One of Esteban and Ximena's brothers, Ismael, and his family would be there with their boat.

Lake Calima was created in the 1940s as part of a hydroelectric project for generating power for the Cauca Valley. At an altitude of almost 5,000 feet and surrounded by mountains, it was a favorite spot for visitors from Cali and Buga, looking for cooler temperatures on the weekends. Windsurfing and water skiing were popular sports, and the tourist industry was growing in the area.

When new family members joined us on our excursions, I tried my best to keep up with all the new names. On this trip, about twelve of us were staying in the rustic cabanas, which had been built originally for the men working on the dam. We brought our own drinking water and showered in cold water. For a day and a half, we went for boat rides, water skied, and looked at the new homes being built on the lake – many in the Swiss Chalet style. We also drove into Darien, a nearby pueblo, and walked around the main square. Later we sat on public benches and watched the people.

The morning was clear and pristine, and the water was smooth as a mirror. At twelve noon, nearly every day, when the winds picked up, the windsurfers came out, creating a colorful panorama on the water. At 6:00 p.m., the winds stopped and clouds rolled in with short spurts of rain. The evening mist that hugged the mountain peaks lasted until the next morning. Again, we ate well and often.

After a full two-day trip, we returned to Cali, tired and sunburned. I couldn't imagine what else this family would have planned for a guest just hoping to learn more about the culture. Over the next few days, we went to Cali Viejo, a restaurant where

I again ate my favorite Colombian dish, *ajiaco.* One night we went to a Salsa club, *El Honka Monka,* and I watched with envy and admiration as my family danced that exciting dance. Xavier was an especially good dancer, but I felt as if I had three feet when I tried to adjust my beach-music rhythm to the Salsa beat. Marta's parents invited us for dinner at their house one night and also to their *finca,* a few miles from Cali one afternoon. We went to local museums and one day drove to the town of Popayán where spectacular ecclesiastical treasures were located. During the times when we were not out, Marta and I stayed in the apartment and talked and relaxed. Friends and relatives stopped by often. She was always accommodating and, even after several days, treated me as if I had just arrived and that I belonged forever. One day before I left, she asked me what my favorite dish was and, of course, I said *ajiaco.* The next day while I was out with Ximena, Marta and the maid prepared the dish, from scratch, and served it that night. Marta was always doing thoughtful things.

One afternoon Ximena showed me a photo album with family pictures from several generations. The group photos reminded me so much of my own family pictures, and I realized how similar our lives were. She told me about her and Rafael's initial failure to get pregnant and, when it didn't happen, that they considered adoption. Her daughters came along, however, before they adopted, and that discussion opened a door for me to talk about my own interest in adopting a child from Colombia.

I had considered adoption for several years. Living with Dot in Bogotá, who had adopted little Lucía, I thought adoption could possibly work for me. Ximena encouraged me and said if I decided to pursue it she could help me. She had family members who were connected to a local orphanage, and she and her mother, Nora, would be my local "supporters," which was required.

I was thrilled to get that information and immediately started thinking about how I could actually start the process. My desire for a child was the basis of my relationship with Ximena. She understood my desire to have my own family and gave me many suggestions and, more importantly, understanding and support. We talked about the possibility of my moving to Cali, and, that day, she asked Xavier to take me by some private schools so I could pick up job applications.

The next day, the day before my return to the States, Xavier drove me to *Colegio* Bennett and *Colegio Bolivar,* two highly regarded private schools in Cali, where summer staff were manning the offices. I was especially impressed with Bolívar, and appreciated the fact that the secretary, a young Colombian woman, took us on a tour of the campus. Before we left, she said, "We are always looking for math teachers and hope you'll send us your application soon." I was thrilled at the prospect of living and working in Cali but tried not to think about it too much yet—there was still one more Friendship Force celebration.

That night the Colombian Friendship Force pulled out all the stops and entertained us lavishly and long at the *Club Colombiano,* a local country club. Decorations on the tables were small Colombian and U.S. flags, flowers everywhere, matchbooks and napkins with the Friendship Force logo. The buffet offered everything from Colombian dishes to fried chicken. Meats, seafood, salads, vegetables, rice, potatoes were creatively arranged, and the aromas were intoxicating. The desserts were luscious. A bar with fruit juices, Coca-Cola, and mixes for alcoholic drinks was set up by the outdoor pool. As a backdrop, music pulled us into the festive and enchanting farewell party. A song by the Colombian singer, Roberto Carlos, *Amigos,* that had become a sort of anthem for the trip, played continuously. As we danced and ate, Xavier and Esteban continued filming. I danced with everyone in our group and hoped my Salsa steps had improved. The night ended with a final rendition of the two national anthems and some of us came close to tears. Americans and Colombians all went home happy and tired and full of benevolence.

Before leaving the next day, Esteban and Marta gave me a copy of the Roberto Carlos record album, which had become synonymous with this trip, with a heartfelt note written on the cover. They also gave me a video on Betamax of the footage Esteban and Xavier had filmed during the exchange. They planned to visit me in North Carolina in August, and we made our final arrangements.

At the airport, Xavier gave me a butterfly, mounted in styrofoam. Maria Isabel and Margarita hugged me, carried my pocketbook, and held my hand until I departed. Ximena and Rafael said they would wait for my return. I was nearly overwhelmed by their expressions of love and friendship. If the other participants had been lucky enough to meet the kind of people I'd met, then the objective of fostering Peace through Friendship was accomplished.

I boarded the plane, pulled out the job application and started making plans to get back to Cali as soon as possible.

Left to right, Rafael Franco, Ximena Franco, Xavier Plata, Esteban Plata, Marta Plata, Margarita Franco (in front). Patricia's Colombian family in Popayán, Colombia, 1982.

PART TWO

Cali

Another Opportunity

This time, it took only eighteen months for me to return to Colombia, and it happened quickly. I didn't know until one month before I left for Colombia that I would accept a new job in Cali, buy a condominium in North Carolina, and make some major changes in my life.

Esteban and Marta came for their visit to New Bern, along with a couple of friends, in August of 1982. At that time, I was living in a small, two-bedroom apartment, but somehow the five of us managed to sleep and eat there for a couple of days and nights before they continued their trip to Raleigh. We wrote letters often, and I also heard from Ximena. Once, Rafael was on a business trip to Boston and called. So, we stayed in touch and they were always asking when I was going to return.

I had accepted a new teaching position in the Craven County Schools at West Craven High School and liked my assignment enough that I was not actively pursuing another one. However, at some point during that school year I filled out the application for Colegio Bolivar and sent it in, hoping to keep my options open. The adoption issue had not gone away, and I explored my choices. As a single parent close to forty years old, I knew my chances of adopting in the States were slim. My romantic life was active, but I didn't see a permanent commitment in my future and knew I wouldn't be able to carry a child out of wedlock and work as a single parent in a small southern town. I also knew I wasn't going to get married just to have a child. So, I kept thinking about adoption and knew that Cali was a possibility.

In addition to having a great job and feeling positive about the future, I purchased a new condominium in New Bern and planned to move in during the Christmas holidays. The closing date was scheduled for early December 1983, and the day before the appointment I received a call from Colegio Bolivar in Cali about a vacancy in their math department. Would I be interested? So, that's how the second job in Colombia came about. With only a few weeks before leaving, I closed on the condominium and turned it over to a realtor to rent, packed up again and moved in with my parents, again, while waiting to leave for Colombia. I had some flexibility with the departure date and chose to leave on January 6, 1984, my fortieth birthday. It seemed appropriate, and I knew I would *always* feel happy when I thought about what I did on my fortieth birthday.

Happy Birthday!

When I called Dan Torlone, the high school principal at Colegio Bolivar, to accept the job, he told me a couple of teachers had an extra bedroom I could rent if I wanted to. That sounded fine. I told Dan my friends would meet me at the airport, and I would call him the next day.

I was scheduled to arrive in Cali at 4 p.m. on Friday afternoon, but when I checked in at the Avianca desk in Miami, my flight was canceled. The next one would leave at 6 p.m., putting me in Cali about 9:30. Exasperated, but with no recourse, I waited, and hoped my friends in Cali called the airport before leaving home.

When I finally boarded, I embraced the familiar Colombian ambience and spent the time thinking about my ultimate objective on this trip. I was well aware that an adoption might not happen. How could I possibly know what obstacles I would encounter? I couldn't, but I was eager to focus on this goal and knew without a doubt that I would explore every possibility. If it didn't happen, then surely something good and valuable would come from the whole experience. I was prepared for either outcome.

When I arrived at 9:30, Ximena, Rafael, and Xavier were there to meet me. They assured me they had called ahead." Don't worry, Patricia, it's not a problem," Rafael said. Xavier quickly picked up my bags, and we were out of the terminal in a heartbeat.

Driving into town with friends on this warm January night, with the windows down and the unique aromas of Cali teasing my senses, I couldn't imagine spending my fortieth birthday in a better way. As the soft breeze soothed my skin, I could feel the tension of the long day slowly dissolve.

Before arriving at the Franco's house, Ximena told me that Esteban and Marta, who had welcomed their new daughter Isabel in November, had separated. Esteban was staying with Ximena and Rafael temporarily and was waiting for us now at the house. Finding that out was disappointing because they were both my friends, and without knowing the circumstances, all I could do was hope they could work things out.

When we entered the house, the first thing I heard was "Happy birthday, Patricia!" and then greetings and hugs from Maria Isabel, Margarita, and Esteban. I was surprised the girls were still awake but Ximena had given them special permission to stay up late for the birthday party. A vase of fresh flowers and a birthday cake were on the table, as well as a bottle of wine and wine glasses for the adults. Pink paper plates and napkins were also on the table. We ate the cake, sipped the wine, and listened to Roberto Carlos on the record player, while talking about this new adventure. They had spoken to Dan Torlone and had agreed on a time for him to come over to meet me. Not a word was mentioned about Esteban and Marta's separation, but I gave him a special hug. Again, these friends had surprised and honored me, and I was sure this was one birthday I would never forget. The next morning, we all got up and went to the river for the day, and I knew I was exactly where I was supposed to be.

On Sunday afternoon, Dan, my principal, came by the house and brought the books and materials for my classes. I knew immediately I'd be able to work with him and looked forward to establishing my place at the school. After he left, I looked at the curriculum guide and notes on the classes. I had taught the Algebra I and Geometry curriculum several times and was getting excited about this new assignment. It would be a different environment and I had positive feelings about the whole arrangement. And besides, the warm, sunny, weather in the dead of winter had boosted my spirits to an incredible level.

New Apartment, New Roommates

Before I arrived in Cali, my two new roommates had both written letters welcoming me and describing the apartment. That helped a lot in terms of packing, and the one electrical appliance they suggested I bring was a toaster oven. Other than that, all I packed was clothes, personal items, linens and a few school materials.

Ximena and Rafael took me to the new apartment building on Monday morning and spoke to the portero, who called the apartment before letting us drive into the parking area. Ximena shuddered when she saw the heavy-duty firearms the two guards were carrying, and I tried to ignore them, while simultaneously telling myself I'd have to deal with these people on a daily basis. If anything, the security issues were just as serious now, if not more so, than when I was in Bogotá. The drug traffic was flourishing in Cali, and crime was rampant. But, somehow, life went on amid the chaos, and I followed the lead of my friends. They didn't ignore the dangers, but they didn't allow the terrorists to control their lives either.

When I found out the apartment was on the eighth floor, I immediately started thinking about walking up all those flights of stairs when the electricity was out. "It will be good for you, Patricia," they laughed, and I had to agree. We made plans to go to

Popayán the following Saturday and said goodbye after getting my suitcases in the apartment.

Jodie and Janet were waiting for me and quickly showed me around. There was a living/dining area and small kitchen (but larger and more modern than the one in Bogotá). In the living room a large window with sliding glass panels opened to a view of Avenida Roosevelt and the mountains in the distance. My bedroom had built-in storage inside the closet, and Jodie and I would share a bathroom. There were two other bedrooms and a second bath at the end of the hall. In the fashion of Colombian homes, the maid's quarters were behind the kitchen and open to a common area where clothes were hung to dry — and also where the maids could socialize during the day by calling out to each other.

"Here's a key for you, Patricia," Janet said as we all sat down on a sofa that had served many import teachers in the past. "We'll take you downstairs and introduce you to the portero, and then, if you'd like, we'll walk over to Cosmocentro and show you around." Cosmocentro was the new shopping center close to our apartment, and I was anxious to go there and get my bearings.

Jodie and Janet apparently knew a lot more about me than I knew about them, but it didn't take long for me to learn about their pasts and get a handle on the situation at school and the apartment. Jody, 27, a fourth-grade teacher, was from Missouri and had taught three years on an Indian reservation in South Dakota. She was short, round, with long, silky, straight blond hair and freckles. Lively and friendly, she was very accommodating. Janet, 30, from Maine, was a vegetarian, and had short, salt and pepper hair. She was also a fourth-grade teacher and had a background in French. A fitness enthusiast, she worked out at the school gym three days a week. She appeared to be rather serious. This was the first overseas teaching job for both of them.

I told them about my plans to adopt, (that information had not been in my application), and also about my Colombian friends in Cali. They seemed to be impressed with both of these facts and wanted to know more. They especially remarked on how lucky I was to have Colombian friends.

Their maid came three days a week and cleaned the apartment and took care of the clothes. They didn't think we would need to hire her for more days. Basically, Monday was wash day, Wednesday ironing day, so I would need to organize my clothes in a certain place if I wanted them washed that week. The routine was similar to the one in Bogotá except we would all be responsible for our own food. Sometimes Mercedes, the maid, would cook rice or make juice, but with different food preferences, Jody and Janet prepared their own meals. That suited me fine since I was determined not to let the weight issue become a problem this time around. We could share the coffee pot in the mornings if I wanted to or just wait until I got to school to eat. It seemed like a workable arrangement for all of us. After finding out their schedules for the mornings and looking around the kitchen, we walked over to Cosmocentro about a block away.

While on our way, they told me the rumor they had heard that our apartment building, Santiago de Cali, was owned by someone in the drug cartel. New and modern, it was typical of many new buildings going up around the city and was, apparently, considered a profitable investment. Whenever there had been a need to call the landlord about a problem in the apartment, the response had been immediate and satisfactory. So, again, there were just certain things we (the expats) had to accept.

The shopping center was very much like the ones in the States: big grocery store, Wal-Mart style department store, clothing shops, beauty parlors, and food kioskos. The only difference was the tight security with guards carrying open firearms surrounding the entrance and parking area.

I grabbed a few items in the grocery store, and after looking around and finding the best place to buy empanadas, we returned to the apartment. I spent the evening unpacking and preparing for work the next day. Jodie and Janet filled me in on Colegio Bolívar (CB), and by 9:30 p.m. I was sound asleep.

When I walked outside the next morning, January 10th, in summer clothes and white shoes, and stood on the corner with Jodie and Janet waiting for the bus, I was nearly overcome with emotion. Whoever heard of anyone getting nostalgic about diesel fumes? There was just something so familiar about the Colombian smells, the sunshine, the traffic, the school children in their uniforms waiting for other buses and the smell of soap. My year in Bogotá came back in a flash, and I was thrilled to be starting out on this new adventure, especially in such a desirable climate. Our bus arrived exactly at 6:30 a.m., and my roommates said Pedro, the driver, had never arrived more than two minutes off that schedule.

That first week at work revealed and prophesied the next eighteen months in the city of Cali. I had a dream schedule: two classes of Algebra I and two of Algebra II, with a total of sixty-seven ninth and eleventh-grade students. With two planning periods, one the first period of the day and one the last period, I had plenty of time to finish most of my work at school. I also had one ten-minute break and a forty-minute lunch period. But the most remarkable thing was my classroom. It had three brick walls with the fourth space open to a view of a pasture where cows grazed and, in the distance, the mountains. On clear days, after the fog lifted, we could sometimes see the snow-covered peaks of the Nevada mountain range, which my students pointed out to me. The grass-emerald green and like velvet-always made me want to take off my shoes. It was invigorating to be in that classroom, especially on those cool mornings with the sun caressing the campus.

My students were charming. One of the guidance counselors told me the first week that the previous teacher had left because of poor student attitudes and discipline problems. She said that she and the administrators were hopeful that with my experience, I could help. I didn't see any signs of those problems and thought it was probably better not to ask too many questions. There was a higher percentage of Colombian students at CB than at CNG in Bogotá, both multicultural and bilingual private schools, and they were absolutely delightful young people; relaxed, funny and well-traveled, as well as focused on their work. They were respectful and seemed eager to please. I hoped I still felt that way in June.

My students at Colegio Bolivar, Cali, 1984.

Since I had missed the orientation for new teachers in August, it took me a while to meet the other faculty members. However, many came by to welcome me, and the Colombian teachers were just as friendly as the import teachers. In fact, one teacher said she had heard I was from North Carolina and said she and her husband were, too. When I asked her where, she said, "Oh, it's a little town I'm sure you've never heard of, Bladenboro."

"Bladenboro? I grew up in Whiteville. So, yes, I know exactly where it is. How did you get to Cali?"

"My husband's a missionary, and we've been here for fifteen years," she told me. "You'll love Cali." Bladenboro was a small town about fifteen miles from Whiteville, and I thought about the coincidence of the three of us ending up here. Several Colombian teachers had attended graduate school at Western Carolina University in the mountains of North Carolina and soon introduced themselves. In fact, one of them, Maria Isabel Rodas, lived with her mother in our apartment building.

That first day, I also met Dr. Martin Felton (he said I could call him Marty), who was the Director of the school. He was intent on strengthening the Math program and wanted to talk to me later about suggestions for moving forward on that level. Jodie and Janet both spoke highly of him.

By the end of the week, I had definitely gotten my feet wet. Teaching in Colombia again was an easy transition, and I didn't expect any adjustment problems. After all, I was in Cali, and I had grown attached to Cali a year earlier. As they say in Cali, "Cali es Cali," as if no other explanation is needed.

Popayan And South Pacific

During the Friendship Force trip of July 1982, I had visited the remote Andean city of Popayán with my friends, the Platas and Francos. I remembered the sun, shade, and churches and a little of the history. This city had acquired great wealth from mining and cattle ranching in the 17th and 18th centuries. With few outlets for extravagance, the families demonstrated piety and affluence by making lavish gifts to the church. Unlike other parts of Spanish America, Colombian artisans had their own traditions of working with gold and did not send to Spain for their offerings. Their proximity to the raw materials-gold, silver and emeralds-meant that they could fashion their own relics. The Popayán treasures became one of the most important and valuable liturgical collections in the world, though not well known.

Each year the church treasures were paraded through the streets during Holy Week, but otherwise they were displayed sparingly. Also, because earthquakes plagued the area and because of the unsettled political conditions, the treasures were often protected in the homes of families who had donated them to the church and were moved frequently. So, that was my memory of Popayán.

And then, on Maundy Thursday, 1983, an earthquake rumbled beneath the city and jerked the earth violently. A creek changed its course, cemeteries spit up corpses, and raw sewage spewed in the streets. Men and animals were thrown to the ground, and the earth opened in places, swallowing everything. After eighteen seconds, the quake was over. About 85 percent of the city was damaged, and at least two hundred and fifty people were killed. More than one thousand were injured, and thirty thousand people lost their homes, fifty-three thousand children were without schools and nearly five thousand businesses were destroyed. All of the churches received major damage.

The news of the earthquake had reached me in the States, and I remembered reading about it, but couldn't imagine the destruction. So, when Ximena and Rafael invited me to go to Popayán again to look at what was left of the city, I eagerly accepted.

Nine months after the earthquake, little restoration had taken place. Rafael maneuvered the car around potholes and debris and pointed out what was left of buildings he had known: the library, a movie theater, apartment buildings. Multi-story structures had collapsed from the bottom, and the interior of many houses could still be seen. Broken furniture, commodes and bathtubs, mud-stained beams were surrealistically strewn around the streets. It was an indescribable and devastating scene. I took pictures and, at the same time, wondered if I really wanted to be reminded of this powerful act of God.

Fortunately, not all was lost in Popayán. The parents of friends of the Francos, who were out of town during the earthquake, had invited us to stop by on our visit. The Londoño family lived in an area that had been spared, and they felt they had been blessed. Speaking no English, they welcomed me profusely in Spanish and chatted away as if I understood everything. The Francos and I had developed our own system of communication, and they instinctively knew when I needed a translation. The Londoños told us about the frescos and religious carvings that had perished in the collapsed churches. However, there was almost daily news about many of the bejeweled altar relics that had survived in different locations. Scholars recorded and photographed these holy works so that the world would become aware of the great cultural heritage that had nearly been lost. The Londoños were passionate about the restoration.

Talk soon turned to food, and when they asked if we would like coffee and a snack, we were grateful. After about thirty minutes, the maid started bringing out tray after tray of *pasabocas* (hors d'oeuvres). It was a feast! Finger food, meat dishes, vegetables, fruit and sweets. We savored the aromas and exquisite tastes. After a while, I stopped asking what the dishes were and just indulged. With the last morsel of food and the last drop of *tinto,* it was time for us to leave and return to Cali. I was greatly moved by the Londoño family and acknowledged this cultural generosity so evident in Colombians. Truly, *"Mi casa es su casa"* had great significance to them.

On the way back to Cali, the two girls sat with Rafael in the front; Ximena and I sat in the backseat.

"I have information about the adoption, Patricia. I talked to someone at Chiquitines, the orphanage, and they said you need to go there. If you'd like me to go with you, I will. I'm not sure they speak much English."

"Yes, of course, Ximena, I'd love for you to go with me," I said. "Is it convenient for you?"

"Yes, I would be happy to help. Can you go next week?" she said. "Maybe Thursday afternoon?"

"Thursday is perfect. Thank you, Ximena," I replied, wishing I could express my gratitude more eloquently.

"Rafael, slow down," Ximena shouted, in Spanish, "you're scaring Patricia. You're driving way too fast." Without a doubt, Rafael drove as if he owned the road, and I was glad to be in the backseat

"Qué maneja? (Who's driving?)" he shouted back and plowed on through the traffic and around the mountains. Ximena just shook her head, and all I could do was smile and cross myself.

"I had a boyfriend one time who drove the same way," I replied. "Used to make me nuts."

"They all want to be Italian race-car drivers in the Grand Prix," Ximena said, and we shared a good laugh.

Sunday was a welcome day of rest in the apartment. I wrote some letters, prepared for my classes and relaxed. Of course, the main thing on my mind was the upcoming trip to Chiquitines. There was nothing I could do at that point to prepare for the visit, so I occupied myself with the other new aspects of my life.

During that first week of school, Dan had talked to me about getting involved in an extra-curricular activity. All teachers were expected to participate in a club or sport, or maybe even establish a new organization, such as Archery or Karate. He said that every two years, the school hired a professional director and produced a play. This was the year for that. Students from all grades participated, but the high school students were the ones who were most involved, mainly because of rehearsal time, and that if I wanted to, I could help with that.

So, on Tuesday afternoon after classes, I showed up at the organizational meeting for "South Pacific." John Palencia, a Colombian who had worked in the theater in New York, was the director. The theater was swarming with kids of all ages-and a lot of parents. "Some Enchanted Evening," "Bali Hai," and other tunes from the Rogers-Hammerstein soundtrack were piped in. Everybody was excitedly talking and moving around. I took a seat on the front row and waited.

When John walked to the front and took the microphone, the kids settled down and gave him their utmost attention. He explained the auditioning process, the roles, rehearsal schedule, and the date of the first performance – Friday, March 29, 1984. That meant two and a half months of total devotion to the project. Auditions for the leading roles would be Saturday, starting at 9:00 a.m. and for the supporting roles of singers and dancers and islanders, at 1:00 p.m. After answering a few questions, John dismissed the group and they scattered quickly.

The adults there came as support personnel, and we were ready to help any way we could. After the students left, Jon asked all of us about our experiences in the theater and said he would let us know our specific assignments soon. "We need ALL of you," he said. "Come to the auditions on Saturday to get a feel for the show."

We talked among ourselves a little, and then Jon came up to me and said, "Patricia, I understand you've just arrived in Cali. Welcome! Thank you for offering to help with the play. Will you be here Saturday?"

"You're welcome. And, yes, I'll be here," I replied, and so began two and a half months that flew by so quickly that, when the play and Easter vacation were behind me, the school year was almost over.

Chiquitines

When Ximena picked me up at the apartment Thursday afternoon, we went straight to Chiquitines. She and her mother, Nora, had already spoken to the director, Berta Lucía Carvajal, on my behalf, and she was waiting for us at the orphanage. We parked in the dirt driveway of a stately old home, which was surrounded by live oak trees, and heard a group of children playing inside the enclosed structure. I was surprised that the walls of an orphanage were topped with broken glass. Ximena spoke to the portero, who apparently was expecting us, and he opened the gate to let us in. To get to the offices, we walked under a covered verandah and noticed a drop in temperature as soon as we entered the house on creaky hardwood floors. Even though we could hear the children outside, the atmosphere was peaceful and calm. On the walls were pictures of orphaned children with their adoptive parent.

Sra. Carvajal greeted us warmly. The first thing she did was say her English was not very good, and I replied that my Spanish was not very good. But, with the three of us having varying degrees of fluency in English and Spanish, we managed to get through that first meeting. The first thing she emphasized was that adoption was not a fast process. It could take years to complete all the required paperwork, and I must not get discouraged. She gave me a packet of instructions to take home and read.

"There will be a lot to do, Patricia. You'll have to submit documents from the States and, in most cases, you'll need originals, not just copies. When you have made some progress with your papers, you can start talking to the children. Then, in time, you can choose a child and start spending time with him or her. First, on a daily basis, and then the child can visit in your apartment for overnight trips. But now, take the list with you and look at it very carefully."

Ximena was translating and explaining what Sra. Carvajal was telling me, and I was astounded at the complexity of the process. After all of my paperwork was approved, then we could start the adoption process, which was even more involved, but which could all be done in Colombia. First, I had to be sanctioned, and that would mean a trip to the States to gather the documents. There was no point in lingering on this first trip, but, before we left, the Director took us on a tour of the house.

In a room with cribs several women were tending to the infants there. In separate quarters the older boys and girls slept several to a room. We saw their dining room and another area where they played inside and did limited learning activities. Most of the time they stayed outside in a well-equipped fenced-in area, and that's where they were when we finished our tour. Several adults were close by. Just back from an afternoon trip to the river, the children were now being hosed down and were squealing with delight. They didn't pay much attention to us that day and seemed to be content.

"Patricia, you can do this," Ximena said, sensing that I was feeling overwhelmed. "It will take time, but it will happen. Did you hear that little boy ask if you were going to be his new mommy?"

I hadn't heard a thing, but that last question moved everything in my mind to an entirely new level. It really could happen, and I slowly started preparing myself for the biggest event in my life, so far.

When I got back to the apartment, Jodie and Janet wanted to know everything I had learned that afternoon, and I was glad they were there. I barely glanced at the packet with the list of things I needed to do. When I finally went to bed, I dreamed of buildings collapsing from the bottom, and mushroom clouds of dust. It was a restless night.

One of the benefits CB provided to the import teachers was membership in a club very close to our apartment. For twenty-five dollars a month the teachers could swim, play tennis or racquetball, enjoy the restaurant and just relax. When I wasn't involved in play practice after school, I often rode the school bus to the club and got off for a quick swim and then walked home. It was a convenient and safe place to go, and I looked forward to the extra exercise.

We also took advantage of the pool at school, which we were allowed to use on the weekends, but that was a longer trip since we had to ride the bus there and back. Also, we had to pack lunches. It became our own version of going to the river, and I thought about how convenient these two places would be when my child arrived. When I wasn't with the Platas and Francos on the weekends, I was usually with a group of teachers at one of the pools.

Janet and her boyfriend, David, had recently bought a jeep and were driving to school each day and around the city a little. They insisted that driving in Cali was not difficult as long as you didn't plan your outings during peak traffic hours. That sounded easy enough to me, and I really started thinking about getting a car. When word got out that I was interested, offers poured in – from teachers who would be leaving at the end of the school year and Colombian teachers who knew somebody who knew somebody who wanted to sell. One such offer came from John, the "South Pacific" director.

One Sunday, he invited me to go with him and a couple of his friends and their baby to see some property he owned where he hoped to build a finca one day. The plan was for us to take a picnic and then look at the foliage to see if there was anything we could use on the set of "South Pacific." He arranged for his helper, called "Hombre," to be there.

Just outside the city, the area was dense and jungle-like. Where a small sloping area was cleared, impatiens spilled down the hill in puffs of color. The foundation of a house from long ago remained, and that's where we spread out our picnic. As John talked about his plans for the house, we ate and relaxed in the shade. A typical Colombian outing. The baby played with some toys and toddled around.

"Okay, let's go look for frangipani," John said as he finished off his beer and started packing up the picnic. He insisted on having real flowers for the set if at all possible. The couple with us decided not to take the baby on the flower search and stayed with the truck at the clearing.

I didn't have a clue about frangipani, but John said to just look for long stemmed plants with multiple flowers. We headed into the jungle with Hombre leading the way, swinging his machete to clear a path through the thick growth. Hombre would hack something down, we'd take a step gingerly, and if we felt safe, continue on. It was impossible to know what we were stepping into, and I was hoping my jeans and sneakers would be enough to protect me from whatever we were getting ready to do. All of a sudden, John let out a startled yell and disappeared into the undergrowth. Hombre, just ahead, immediately turned around, let out his own yell, and jumped into the spot where John was last seen. I could hear both of them shouting and cursing as they hacked at branches until finally, John reappeared, scratches on his face and barely able to stand. Apparently, he had stepped into a hole, which was impossible to see, fell down and got tangled up in the vines and growth, and sprained his ankle. Struggling to walk and leaning on Hombre, he was pissed.

So, there was no frangipani that day, and I decided if he asked me again to go with him, I'd politely decline. Soon we made it back to the truck, sat down and rested. There was one beer left, and we all decided that John should have it. Eventually, all was well again, and we left the future finca site and returned to Cali. During the ride back, we were talking about his truck, and he said, "I can't imagine not having a truck. There's always something I need to carry or pick up, and a car just wouldn't do for me. Do you plan to get a car"?

"I'm looking into it," I replied, "It would make a big difference, but I probably won't do anything right away. Maybe after "South Pacific" I'll have time to look around."

With that little bit of information, he told me about someone who had a 1974 Nissan jeep for sale for $3,000. "I'll have him call you soon," he said.

"Okay, but I'm probably not going to get anything until school is out," I said.

Within a week, the seller had called and come to the apartment for me to take the car for a test drive. I was not planning to buy a car anytime soon and tried to make that clear. Not taking "no" for an answer, he continued to call until finally I mentioned something about it at school. Almost immediately, Marty (Dr. Felton) called me into his office, told me he knew the seller AND the car, and that I didn't need to be involved with either one. He assured me I wouldn't be bothered by this person anymore, and that took care of the problem. Another example of the way the school offered a helping hand. He also told me that the school had two cars that were available for teachers to rent, and anytime I needed one for a weekend to just let him know. That welcome bit of information solved my car problems for a while.

Bombs, Explosions And
How To Mail Cheese

My parents were both retired at this time, and their letters arrived with regularity. They reported that my sisters and nieces and nephews were all fine. Shannon, the niece who had baked a cake for my farewell party with the Colombian flag for icing, was getting ready to graduate from college with a degree in Marine Biology. Stephanie, Mike and Travis were all growing up and showing signs of artistic and musical abilities. Aunts, uncles and cousins were all doing fine, too. In one letter, Mother told me that teachers in North Carolina would receive a fifteen percent raise for the coming year. I think she told me that in an effort to get me to return home at the end of the school year. It was tempting, but I felt as if I had barely arrived in Cali and I hadn't come close to meeting my objective, yet. They occasionally sent packages with clothing and food. The things I really wanted, though, like milk and cheese, couldn't be sent through the mail – until Jodie told me how her parents had sent cheese from Wisconsin straight to Cali. Here's what she said.

"Buy a big block of the Carrel extra sharp cheddar, which comes in a heavy-duty wrapper. Then wrap it in paper towels, then saran wrap, then aluminum foil, and then just put it in a big envelope. That's all there is to it."

"That's true," Janet said, "I saw it and couldn't believe it didn't melt or turn green with mold."

When I sent my parents the instructions, I guess they were skeptical because I never received cheese that way. I kept the instructions, however, just so I could try it someday when I returned to the States.

I had met people I was happy to spend time with, and one of the teachers, Dan, became a surrogate Jerry to me. He even looked a little like Jerry with his muscular build and dark hair. So far as I know, he wasn't dating anybody in Cali, but I think he would have liked to. Romance was definitely not a part of our relationship, but he would go places with me, sit with me at lunch and help whenever I needed help. When "South Pacific" rehearsals became more frequent, Dan would often return to school with me for a night practice. We'd ride the Blanco y Negro bus line, and then John would bring us home, sometimes as late as 11:00 p.m.

One afternoon a couple of weeks before opening night, I left the apartment to return to the school for practice. That week I was working with choreography for the "Bloody Mary" segment, and, for the first time all dancers would be there. Dan had stayed at school that afternoon, so I was going to the bus stop alone. To get there I had to walk around the shopping center and cross over to the back side where the bus stopped. As I approached Cosmocentro, I noticed smoke suddenly billowing out of the building. Then people, a few at first, and then many, were running outside and away from the building. I didn't see anyone who appeared injured, but they all seemed frightened. Someone was shouting "bomba," and I knew immediately there had been an explosion inside the center. At that point, I was closer to the bus stop than the apartment and fled as quickly as possible to the pick-up area. A bus pulled up as soon as I got there, and I got on board, with several others fleeing the scene, and took a seat. People were shouting, and I could tell they were angry. Many of them lived in constant fear of groups like FARC and the ELN, and they were sick of the disruptions caused by these groups. I often wondered where the strength came from that allowed them to move forward and not give in or give up.

The next day, an article in the newspaper reported that FARC took responsibility for the bombing at Cosmocentro. Terrorist activity had increased recently, and the paper said that FARC was planning more disruptions during the upcoming *Semana Santa*

(Easter or Holy Week). When that report came out, the school immediately told us to cancel any vacation plans we had for travel around the country that week and to be extremely careful if we had to move around the city. But, before we reached that point, we had a play to produce and one more week of school after that.

With preparations for the play in high gear and the terrorist activity so rampant, one would expect tensions at school to be high. Being able to concentrate on academics seemed unlikely, but that's exactly how everybody dealt with the uncertainty. There truly was nothing we could do but move forward.

At play practice, the students who were not involved in a stage scene worked on their homework. The teachers tutored when someone needed help. The thirteen-member orchestra came in to practice with the students and sets went up. A waterfall, beach scene and frangipani appeared, and coffee pots gurgled. In the middle of all of this was John, directing, suggesting, yelling, and a play was created.

On opening night, with orchestral strains of "Some Enchanted Evening" wafting out the doors and windows of the auditorium, John and I climbed a ladder to the balcony, where the console for the lights was, and flicked the lights five minutes before curtain. Almost magically, people sat down, the orchestra changed tunes, and the stage came to life. The lights went down and then up again, and when the curtain opened, we were transported to the South Seas hacienda of Emile de Becque, where his two children were playing and then singing "Dites-Moi."

The auditorium was filled to capacity for the two weekends and six nights, bolstering our spirits beyond belief. If anybody ever questioned the wisdom of continuing with the play in the face of unknown dangers, it wasn't those nights. The administration and parents based their decision on years of experience and their concern about the welfare of the entire Colegio Bolivar family. In addition, John had inspired the students to professional quality work, and I was sure their achievements would strengthen their confidence and bring a sense of accomplishment to them for the rest of their lives. What a success!

The wrap party after the last performance was held at a finca close to the school owned by the family of two of our students. The son, Ernesto, had one of the lead roles in the play as Lt. Joseph Cable, USMC, and the daughter, Christina, kept us supplied with brownies and cookies during rehearsals. In fact, she had established a successful catering business at school. Once when I ordered a cheesecake from her for a dinner party we were having at our apartment, her father, who was divorced, brought the cake to me at the apartment and stayed to visit a while. I had also seen him on a few other occasions and thought he was friendly and handsome. My interest was piqued.

When we arrived at their house late that night, the side of the mountain was lit up with spotlights like a bonfire. Once past tight security, John and Dan and I were shown to a living area where comfortable chairs were placed around a fire and all the glass doors were open. Several adults were talking and enjoying drinks and food. Our host, whom I had looked forward to seeing, was attentive. A swimming pool, visible from inside, was built into the side of the mountain. A stairway led down to an underground sitting area where an observer could watch people swimming. Like an aquarium, I thought. Dan thought it was kinky, and I could see that, too. So far as I know, no one was watching any underwater antics at that time. The students had started their own celebration and were swimming, dancing, and eating, all against a backdrop of loud, throbbing salsa music. The adults at the party, parents included, looked the other way.

The party lasted for the rest of the night and by the time the sun came up, John had disappeared. I was anxious to get back to my apartment, and the owner offered to have one of his drivers take me and a couple of other people home. The students were scattered around the grounds, and I imagine they slept most of the day. It had been a long run, and I was ready to get some distance between me and "South Pacific."

We returned to classes for one more week before the ten-day vacation and then the final push for the end of the school year.

Boy Or Girl?

During the vacation I saw my Colombian friends a few times and was glad that Esteban and Marta were back together. I finally met their beautiful little daughter, Isabel Cristina, and on one of our day trips, we rode to Lake Calima. I didn't tell anybody where we were going since teachers were advised not to leave the city, because I felt safe with them and knew they would not put me in any danger. We visited with Esteban's brother and his family, the ones who had taken us skiing during the Friendship Force visit. It was a cool but sunny day, and I was glad I had taken a heavy sweater. As we drank coffee and walked around their property, Esteban said he was hoping to build his own vacation house here someday, right on the waterfront. When he pointed out some areas where he might be able to do that, I thought, it's just a matter of time; one day he'll have his house here.

    During this vacation time, Dan and I went to Northside Pizzeria a couple of times, and Janet, David, Jodie and I walked over to Cosmocentro for groceries. One night I woke up to the sound of horses' hooves and voices and knew I wasn't dreaming. I got up and looked out the window and could see dozens of people on horses moving down the street. The next day, my roommates told me that the Indians came down from the mountains when FARC put them in danger, and they passed through the city at night to avoid the traffic. It wasn't the last time I heard the Indians. We were close enough to the club that we swam a few times for some exercise. Janet and I had bought a 17" black and white TV and tried to watch it but without much success. Somebody said the mountains caused the poor reception. Other than that, I spent my vacation time resting, reading and writing.

Finally, I read the adoption paperwork from the orphanage and started making plans. It was obvious I would have to return to the States for the majority of the papers, and that meant I needed to start immediately on my *Paz y Salvo* so that I could leave Colombia in late June. That was at the top of my list but I couldn't proceed until we returned to school. I also had to think about housing for the coming year since having a child would require a different arrangement, including a live-in maid. At least the car situation was not pressing, and I planned to rent one from school soon to experiment. Janet and Jodie had not made definite plans for the coming year other than a commitment to returning, but they were both thinking of trying new living arrangements, so we had the opportunity to discuss all of the possibilities.

I had time to write my parents about the trip to Chiquitines. Mother knew of my interest in adoption, but we had never really discussed it in detail. She didn't act shocked or surprised but was just rather noncommittal. I knew we would talk more when I got home for the summer. Here's the list I sent to her of some of the things I would have to round up:

1. Divorce decree (not the settlement)
2. Deed to the property I owned in New Bern
3. A copy of my Social Security card
4. A letter from my doctor stating I was in excellent general health
5. W-2 statement from '83
6. Letter from the bank stating that I had good credit
7. Recent work history before coming to Cali, complete with references

From Cali, I would need a certified copy of my contract at Colegio Bolivar, copies of the *Paz y Salvo, Cedula (ID card),* passport, and letters from Ximena and Nora testifying to my character and fitness as a mother. It was a long list, and I knew the process would take time, but I was totally committed and ready to get started. During the last few weeks of school, I delved into my school work and final activities.

One Sunday night a call from the portero in our apartment building reported a bomb threat on the fifth floor. We evacuated immediately and spent a few hours outside while everything was searched. FARC took responsibility for the call, but we were never able to determine if a bomb was found. Another theory involved the rumor that the Cali Cartel owned our building and did a lot of big-time drug trafficking from a fifth-floor apartment. The theory implied that the police often reported bombs so they could search apartments without getting search warrants when they suspected drug activity. Getting innocent bystanders out of the building usually meant fewer injuries in case of any trouble, so they reported bombs. It was anybody's guess who was really responsible, but our biggest threat was that we tended to get blasé about the dangers.

I lost one of my contact lenses and went to Optica Aleman for a replacement. They said it would take about eight days to get a new one, and at the end of three weeks it still hadn't arrived.

CB sponsored a "Spirit Week" for the first time, and it was a huge success. For a part of each day, the entire high school was involved in team and individual activities, as well as class competitions. On "Sports Day" the sophomore class, which was my homeroom, won the prize. There were other activities those last weeks and as we approached the week of final exams, a calm wind fell over the campus, and everybody got serious. Students took exams in the gymnasium, which was open-air with rows of desks lined up. All math exams were scheduled at the same time, so the different math teachers proctored with guidance counselors or assistants. This method was used for all the subjects and worked well.

During exam week I received a call at school from Chiquitines. Sra. Carvajal asked if I could come to the orphanage and, of course, I said yes. On the following afternoon I rode the school bus to our meeting. After a cup of tinto and a small cookie in her office, she asked how I was progressing with the paperwork. I reported that I did not anticipate any problems getting the documents, but it would be at least a month before I went to the States. I would bring everything to her as soon as I got back. Then she asked if I would prefer to adopt a boy or girl. I truly had not given much thought to a preference and told her that it didn't matter. What was important was that the child be reasonably healthy because, as a single working parent with a single income, providing care for a handicapped child would be difficult. She had told me earlier that, because of my age, (I was forty), that I should adopt a child at least six years old, and I was prepared for that. I also told her I would like to have a child who could matriculate in school, since he or she would be going to Colegio Bolivar with me until I returned to the States. Before ending our meeting, she said that someone from Bienestar, similar to Social Services in the States, would contact me for an interview as soon as I turned in my paperwork and it was verified. I was excited and almost giddy with the prospect of the adoption truly happening soon. As I left the orphanage, I spotted a group of children playing outside and noticed that nearly all of them had distended stomachs, typical of malnourished children.

My teacher friends were supportive with each bit of news about the adoption, and my Colombian friends were ecstatic. After graduation, faculty wrapped up the school year with farewell parties and goodbyes. Some would be leaving Cali permanently, and others would return for the next school year. Jodie had decided to move in with two other teachers who were good friends, and Janet and I decided to continue living in the same apartment. My child would have Jodie's room, and I would pay two-thirds of the expenses when he or she moved in, and we would look for a live-in maid when the time came. Dan, my principal, and Marty, the director, both thanked me for the job I was doing and shared several ideas for the math department in the coming year. I was looking forward to contributing any way I could.

Before we left for vacation, the school arranged a trip to Ginebra, a town about an hour's drive from Cali, for one night of the Mono Nuñez Music Festival. Composers and interpreters come from all over the country to participate and compete in a three-day event of non-stop Andean music. The emphasis is on the fusion of traditional and modern music, but our night there we heard strictly traditional music played on traditional instruments. The *tiple,* which has four sets of three strings, was one of the instruments used during the concert and is considered the rhythmic backbone of the

Andean tunes. The haunting melodies and cool mountain air that night created a mysterious and ethereal mood.

The name of the festival comes from Benigno Nuñez, whose nickname was "Mono" meaning "monkey." He specialized in the *bandolo*, a small pear-shaped stringed instrument, similar to a mandolin. Many instruments and handicrafts were displayed, along with a book fair, and food from the Cauca Valley. We had time to walk around and look at everything and eat some excellent empanadas. Before leaving, I bought a colorful poster of an Andean musician playing a flute made from the sugar cane, inscribed with words from Igor Stravinsky extolling the virtues of tradition.

Mom's Visit

My summer visit to North Carolina was full of the normal activities I usually took care of when I returned home: trips to the doctor and dentist, time with my nieces and nephews and other family members, a quick trip to New Bern, a visit with my best friend Marilyn and her family in Saluda outside Asheville, and, of course, a few trips to the beach. My mother's brother, Harry, and his wife Berniece, lived in Myrtle Beach and were especially interested in the adoption. Recently retired, Harry had always had an interest in the Spanish language and Latin American culture. In fact, a few years earlier, he, Berniece, Mother and I took a trip to Mexico City where he had a chance to practice his Spanish. So, he wanted to know everything, and I told him what I could. He reminded me that if there was anything he could do to help, he would be glad to, and I knew he meant it. Little did I know at that time how instrumental his efforts would be in getting my child to the States.

With time, I was able to find all the papers I needed and made many trips to the library to get notarized copies. I searched through my closet for summer clothes and went shopping for shoes, which were hard to find in Cali. I desperately wanted to buy clothes and toys for my child but held off since I didn't have enough information yet.

Mother surprised me one day by saying, "I'll go back with you, if you don't mind, and spend a couple of weeks. I'd like to see Cali."

"Of course! I'd love for you to come and stay as long as you can. Janet and Jodie will be on vacation, we have room, and it will be a perfect time. We go back to work around the middle of August, so we'll have time to do whatever you want to do. The Platas and Francos have been waiting for you to visit."

To be honest, I wasn't entirely surprised when she said that because my mother always knew instinctively when someone in the family needed some special support. We hadn't talked much about the adoption, but she knew I was serious and that it was probably going to happen. So, she was showing her love and concern by volunteering to travel to Colombia to help. Daddy would have liked to go, too, but at seventy-four, he wasn't sure he was up to the trip physically. Mother, however, at sixty-nine, seemed to grow younger each day and delighted in choosing her clothes and packing her suitcase.

The Platas and Francos all met us at the airport when we arrived in Cali. There were introductions and a lot of hugs and kisses. The children, as usual, were beautiful and loving. Even the baby, Isa, smiled at Mom.

Mom's name was Rachel, and they gave it the Spanish pronunciation. "Raquel, did you feel the earthquake?" Rafael asked. Neither one of us had felt an earthquake. "It was a special gift just for you." He explained that just as we were landing, a small tremor had occurred, and he wanted to make sure that Mother knew it was an announcement to Colombia that she had arrived. She quickly picked up on his sense of humor and fell in love with my Colombian friends.

Esteban drove us to the apartment, and we made plans to see them in a couple of days. Janet and I had arranged to go on vacation at different times during the summer so that the apartment would not be empty for long. She and David made their plans to be there the night we arrived and were planning to leave the next day on their trip. When Mother and I arrived, they had prepared a hot meal for us, and all we had to do was sit down and eat. Mom was tired, so after our meal and a little unpacking, she turned in. Janet and David caught me up on the news around the city and gave me their upcoming itinerary. There were boxes stacked up in the corner of the living room that Jodie planned to pick up when she returned. Janet also told me some disturbing news about the father of Ernesto and Cristina, who had hosted the cast party for "South Pacific."

She knew there had been a spark of interest between us, and she gently told me that he had died about ten days earlier of a cerebral hemorrhage. It was shocking to everyone because he seemed to be in excellent health. With that sad news, I thanked Janet and David both for preparing the meal and went to my bedroom. The day had suddenly gotten much longer.

Janet and David were up and out early the next morning, and by the time Mom got up, it was almost 9:00 a.m., late for her. Janet had made sure there was enough food in the refrigerator to last a couple of days, so we had a leisurely breakfast. It was mid-July, and Mom was accustomed to air-conditioning at this time of the year, but there was no need for it in the apartment. She was wearing a sweater, and she praised the beautiful weather in Cali.

"It's like this all the time," I said. "Sometimes during the day, if you're out in the sun, it gets really hot, but once you step in the shade, you don't feel the heat. And when the breeze picks up in the afternoon, it's delightful and refreshing. Even when it rains, it's not uncomfortable. This is one of the reasons I'm so attached to this place."

"I can see why," she replied, as she looked out the window at the hills in the distance, still enshrouded in a soft morning mist.

We eventually walked over to Cosmocentro where I picked up a few groceries. I had tried to prepare her for the armed guards all along the way, but the reality of seeing men in fatigues carrying machine guns still came as a shock. I suggested that she not stare, just as I suggested that she wear simple clothes and no, or very little, jewelry. The whole idea was to be as inconspicuous as possible. We had a cup of cappuccino at an outdoor restaurant, and she finally had a chance to eat one of my favorite Colombian foods, *pan de bono.* She wasn't disappointed. After walking around the mall we returned to the apartment where Mother rested while I prepared our evening meal.

Before a simple dinner of baked chicken, rice and a salad, we had a glass of wine and tried to watch the news on TV. Since the reception was so poor, I turned it off and we just talked. She opened the conversation, and we had our first real discussion about the adoption.

Always gentle, always kind, she asked, "Why do you want to adopt a child? What has happened to cause you to make this decision?"

Trying to be honest, with her as well as myself, I said "Mom, I'm forty years old, and I'm not even dating anybody I would consider marrying right now. So it's not likely that I'm going to have a child the normal way, and this is an option."

"But why do you want a child?" she persisted.

"I suppose for the same reasons anybody else wants a child. One day I'll be glad to have someone around and to have my own family. There's just something missing, and I think that's what it is," I replied. "I know it's not going to be easy to do this alone, but I think I can. And I want to do it."

"You know that children are expensive, and there will be days you'll be so tired you'll wonder why you went through with this. Especially as a single, working parent. I just hate to see you take on more than you should," Mother offered.

"I know, but haven't people done this for all eternity? How can anybody know what parenthood is like until they've tried it? I feel like I have an advantage because of my age, and I don't think I'm going into it blindly," I said. "Do you think I'm being selfish to want my own child?"

"Not at all, and you'll make a wonderful parent." A slight pause, a sip of wine, and then, "I'm getting a little hungry. Is it time to eat, yet?"

We enjoyed a good meal and connected in the way that only mothers and daughters can when they're on the same wavelength. All was well.

The next day, Marta, Esteban and little Isa picked us up at 2:00 p.m. for a trip to the club Tequendama. On the way there Esteban drove by Chiquitines so I could leave my carefully prepared documents with Sra. Carvajal. I ran in quickly and left them with the secretary since the Director was not there. We spent the afternoon swimming in the pool and relaxing under the cabanas. I took some pictures and, in one of Mom, she was sitting under the cabana, the sun was caressing her shoulders, the wind was blowing her hair gently and she was beautiful. It was exquisite, and I was so glad she had come for a visit. When we returned to the apartment about 6 p.m., we enjoyed a quiet evening.

The next morning, Xavier picked us up about 10:00 a.m. and we headed out to Sylvia, one of my favorite towns. This is where the Indians lived who wore the distinctive purple and pink ruanas, and I knew Mom would enjoy seeing them. We rode in his open-air jeep for a couple of hours, and I was glad I had reminded Mom to wear something warm. As we ascended the mountain, the terrain became more rugged, and I watched Mom carefully to make sure she was comfortable.

Before walking around town, we stopped for lunch in a restaurant that appeared to be someone's house. Xavier said they served excellent *sancocho,* that hearty, delectable potato soup. They must have made it from scratch because, by the time it arrived, we had been waiting for over an hour and Mom was getting weak. It turned out to be well worth the wait, and we all filled our bowls twice and finished off a loaf of homemade bread.

We drove from the restaurant to the town square where Xavier parked the jeep so he could keep an eye on it. Indians milled around in their colorful outfits and we walked to the market to look at their displays of food and handicrafts. Mom bought a few trinkets, and then we entered a building where women were weaving the cloth used for the ruanas. The looms were humming and babies sat on the floor beside the adult women. Mom examined everything respectfully and seemed to be thrilled at what she saw. When we walked to the river and saw the women washing clothes with the children close by, I asked if I could take a picture, and they graciously nodded their heads. I took a few pictures of Mom standing beside them, and, at five feet two inches tall, she towered over the tiny women. In one shot, she was crouched down beside two children on the bank of the river, with her arms around their shoulders, and she looked as happy as I had ever seen her. There was just something magical about the sun and cool temperatures on the banks of the river.

Mom and Patricia with two Indian women in Sylvia, July 1984.

After more sightseeing we returned to Cali and had a light dinner at the apartment. Xavier had been a considerate and accommodating guide taking us to Sylvia.

Every day during Mom's visit we had some special activity. The next day went to the school where I cashed a check for pesos and picked up the car that I had rented for a couple of weeks. When we rode the *blanco y negro* bus out there, Mom commented that she hadn't ridden a public bus since she was in college at Greensboro. The campus of Colegio Bolivar is beautiful, and she was just as captivated as I was. No matter how hot it might get during the daytime, one could always find a cool spot to sit down and relax. Lush and verdant, it's an inviting place and she said she couldn't believe it was a school. A retired educator herself, she was impressed. I showed her my classroom and pointed out the view I had of the mountains and then walked by the pool and gymnasium and soccer field. Before picking up the keys to the car, I introduced her to the summer staff, who treated her like a queen.

I had driven the car before in a practice run and was looking forward to having access to it. A small Renault, with five forward gears in the dashboard, it was easy to handle, but lacked seatbelts. I had become so accustomed to them in the States that I felt unshackled. Our first stop was a small outdoor restaurant where Mom had her first empanadas with chimichurri sauce, which she liked very much. We also had a beer, not her usual drink, but which accompanied the empanadas so well. At the grocery store I loaded up on items that were difficult to carry in my backpack, and when everything was packed in, we went home. The beer had made both of us sleepy so, after a few trips in the elevator carrying the groceries up to the eighth floor, we took long naps.

Later in the afternoon, Mom was still in her room. When I looked in on her, she was sleeping soundly. Trying to be quiet so as not to wake her, I went to my room and started putting up clean clothes the maid had left on the dresser. I still needed to store things I had brought back from the States. Very quietly I moved my desk chair to the closet so I could reach the top shelf. I picked up several items, stepped up on the chair, and started putting them away. Suddenly, I started feeling light-headed and grabbed the shelf to balance myself. For a moment the sensation subsided, and then it came back with a vengeance. I realized immediately we were having a temblor and hoped it was not a full-fledged earthquake. I heard the maids yelling in the laundry area and flew into Mother's room to get her up and out of the building. The electricity was the first thing to go during these temblores, so everybody ran for the staircase. Mother had awakened after the first shock and said it felt like a wave rolling under the bed. As we started down the stairs amid a lot of terrified people, I was concerned for her well-being. She seemed to be fine, though, and we made it down with no problems. After an hour, we were told it was safe to return to our apartment, and we started the long trek up eight flights of stairs. If I could have carried my mother, I would have, but we took our time, and she was in good shape when we got back to our place. She made a joke about Rafael's reference to the first temblor on the day she arrived, and said she now felt very welcome in Colombia.

Mother had a chance to tell Rafael just that the next day when Ximena, Rafael, and their girls picked us up for a trip to visit an aunt and uncle who lived in the country. Rafael and my mother were developing a good relationship, and I was happy to see her so engaged.

The finca we visited reminded me of a smaller version of *Piedechinche*, the sugar-cane hacienda we had seen during the Friendship Force trip. The couple welcomed us warmly. My parents' age, they spoke no English, but made it clear that "their home was our home." We sat in the shade on the verandah and talked, as best we could, and watched the girls play with some cousins in the velvet grass. The children of the couple who provided security and housekeeping were also playing with the group.

After a while, Maria Isabel came running out of a shed and shouted, "Patricia, Raquel, come. Kittens!" Mother and I walked to the barn, with Maria Isabel holding Mother's hand. Inside, the children were squealing and squirming around a box where four kittens were nursing. The mama cat was patiently watching the children and warned anyone who strayed too close with a swat of her paw. The kids were enthralled, and so were we. Eventually we left the barn and walked back to the house, escorted by all the children.

When the meal was ready, Mother and I were led to the kitchen along with Rafael and three other people. We sat at a round table that held six comfortably. The others were eating in the living room and I had the sense that we were given seats of honor. The first course was fried green platanos served with *hogado,* a sauce of finely chopped onion and tomato, mixed with oil, and *hojaldras,* little pastries made of water, flour and egg, fried in oil and sprinkled with sugar. Mother devoured this quickly. When Rafael noticed *how* quickly, he said, "Raquel, there is more." Soon, the main dish was brought to the table. *Sancocho,* that hearty soup typical of the Cauca Valley cuisine, made with chicken, green platanos, yucca, corn on the cob, and cilantro, was served in steaming bowls. A little different from the *sancocho* we ate in Sylvia, but *sancocho,* nonetheless. When Mother tasted it, she closed her eyes gently, shook her head slowly, and let out a long sigh of appreciation. Soon, empty bowls were whisked away, and plates of white rice, pieces of chicken, salad with avocados, and more fried platanos with the *hogado* sauce were placed on the table. We paced ourselves and tasted it all. By the time we got to the dessert, *melado,* another typical Valley dish, made with *panela,* brown sugar derived from the sugar cane, and served with *cuajada,* a mild white cheese, we were barely picking at our food. We didn't want to leave anything unsampled. We truly received a magnificent feast.

Soon after finishing that delectable meal, Ximena told us that everybody would now take a siesta. She led Mother and me to a bedroom where the covers on two single beds had been turned down. Soft quilts that appeared to be handmade were folded at the bottom of each bed. The shutters on the windows kept out the afternoon sun and the room was cool. Before leaving us for our nap, she showed us the bathroom where two toothbrushes were placed on the tile countertop with a tube of toothpaste nearby. "For you," she said.

"Ximena, thank you and please tell your aunt and uncle we thank them, also," I said.

"It's our pleasure," she replied.

Amazed at the hospitality, Mother lay down on her bed. We both slept at least an hour. After a restful nap, we freshened up and returned to the verandah where we smelled the strong, enticing aroma of Colombian coffee. We woke up with cups of tinto and chatted with our hosts. After more expressions of gratitude, we headed back to Cali. The food, the nap, and the peaceful countryside had made us all mellow.

We rested the next day and watched a little television. Mom couldn't translate the Spanish but understood a lot just by listening to the tones in the voices and seeing the pictures. Later in the afternoon, she noticed the fires burning in the mountains. FARC set fires in the sugar cane fields to make some political points. I had grown so used to seeing them that I barely noticed them anymore.

We had a few more excursions to make, and the next one was a fashion show at the Hilton Hotel. We invited Marta and Ximena to go and treated them to the afternoon. On a girls' day out, we had a lot of fun.

Another afternoon, Esteban and Ximena's mother, Nora, and Aunt Cila, treated us to lunch at Esteban's pizzeria. Marta and Isa, with Ximena and her two daughters, joined us for another day of fellowship and good food.

Mother had heard me talk about Lake Calima, and when Esteban and Marta asked if we'd like to ride up there one day, we jumped at the chance. When we arrived at the lake, Esteban, who was still thinking about his future house there, showed us where he hoped to build it. The weather was especially cool that day, and we wrapped up well with sweaters and socks. We visited with Esteban's brother and his family again and spent a couple of hours just eating, talking and walking around the property. When the fog rolled in over the lake that afternoon, I was glad Mom had the chance to see the breathtaking sight. She was beginning to understand the pull Cali had on me. I was content there, and she sensed it.

Before she returned to North Carolina, Mom wanted to do something special for my friends, who had automatically become her friends. She was so grateful for all they had done and so humbled by their generosity that she wanted to express her appreciation. We decided to treat them to a dinner at a well-known restaurant called Cali Viejo.

Cali Viejo was a sprawling finca on the banks of the Cali River. Built in 1870, it catered to no more than twenty-five guests at a time, serving traditional foods in a relaxed atmosphere. A fireplace and indoor/outdoor patio dining provided the ambience which I associated with Cali and wanted to share with Mom. Even the waiters were dressed in clothes from the nineteenth century.

Esteban, Marta, and Xavier picked us up at the apartment, and we met Ximena and Rafael at the restaurant. Everybody was dressed more formally than usual, in honor of Mother's visit and our friendship with the Platas and Francos. Beef dishes were the entrees of choice that night, and all came with a variety of soups and salads. While we were eating, a musical trio playing traditional Andean music stopped beside Mother's chair to serenade her. She was glowing. The helpings were enormous, and when it came time for dessert, we ordered only four and passed them around. Mother had no problem communicating with my friends; the basic qualities of kindness and respect need no translation. They fell in love with her and she with them. The wonderful evening was a fitting end to her trip to Colombia. I think she accomplished her mission.

We spent the next day preparing her things for the return flight and talking about the coming year. There was a chance I'd be going to the States for Christmas, but that was not definite. Probably, I'd be returning permanently next summer, along with my child, and would be going back to work. My mother encouraged me to come home because she knew I needed to contribute to the North Carolina retirement system, especially with a new dependent. I had a lot to think about, and she tried to help me sort through it all. At the shopping center I picked up empanadas for our dinner and also ripe papayas and mangos, which she especially liked. After a light meal, we turned in early, in anticipation of her crack-of-dawn departure.

Esteban had volunteered to take Mom to the airport, and, of course, I was also going. She had no problems getting through immigration, and we chatted and hugged as long as we could. When Mother turned and gave that final wave, I was suddenly transported to that day in August of 1975, on my first flight to Colombia, when I walked across the tarmac in Wilmington and turned and waved to her and Daddy. Those familial bonds were still tight.

For some reason, her flight was delayed for over an hour, and Esteban was worried. In Colombia, one has many opportunities to worry, and we stood in the terminal watching her plane, wondering if she would be getting back off. Eventually, it taxied down the runway and made a smooth departure, and we kept an eye on it until it disappeared in the clouds. Later, she told me that inside the plane, she couldn't understand what the stewardesses were saying, but she knew from the reaction of the other passengers there was some tension. They arrived safely in Miami, and she eventually reached North Carolina. I was greatly relieved when she called to say she was home.

AUGUST 1984 –
JUNE 1985

August 1984

Soon after Mother left, I drove to the school to get a copy of my contract for Chiquitines and to start the paperwork for my *Paz y Salvo,* in case I decided to go home for Christmas. While I was there, Marty asked me to come to his office.

"Patricia, I have a couple of things I want to ask you about, but first, how are things going with the adoption?"

"Well, I turned in my paperwork to the office as soon as I got back from the States, and, so far as I know, everything's in order," I said. "One of the things I need to get today is a copy of my contract. So, I'm hoping to hear something soon."

"You know, I've been in Cali for several years and have known a lot of people who adopted Colombian children. If there's anything that seems to be consistent, it's that it always takes longer than you think. It's a complicated process, so don't get discouraged when you think they've forgotten all about you. Also, we'll be here to help any way we can," he offered. "I don't know either if anybody has told you, but when you do adopt the child, he or she will be able to attend school here. Adopted children are entitled to all the benefits of a person's own biological children, and that certainly includes enrollment at the school. You can ride the bus together, and that has always worked out well for teachers who come here with school-age children."

"Thank you, Marty. Having your support means a lot, and really, the support of everybody who knows I'm trying to adopt here has been incredible," I replied.

"Okay, the other things I wanted to ask you about are: one, we're planning to offer an SAT prep course to our seniors and wonder if you would be interested in teaching the math part. We'll have materials you can follow, and it will meet two afternoons a week for six weeks. There will be a small stipend if you agree to do it."

"Of course," I replied, thinking about the few extra pesos and also the chance to work with the seniors who signed up for the course. "I'd love to. When will it meet?"

"October into November. The SAT test is before Thanksgiving."

"I can't think of any reason not to, so count me in."

"Great. I've heard good things about your work, and I think you can do a good job. The other thing involves the new teachers coming on August 9th. Could you come out for their orientation on the 14th? Just talk to them and help answer questions?"

"I'll be glad to. If there's anything special you'd like me to say, just let me know."

"And one more thing. Once school starts, if there's not much demand for the car from the other teachers, we might work out a lease arrangement for the year," he offered.

"Sounds great. It's an easy car to drive, and I have really enjoyed having access to it. Thanks!"

With that, I picked up the copy of the contract and walked to the car with an extra bounce. There was nothing quite like getting that nod of approval from your boss.

Before going home, I planned to run a couple of errands, one of which, fortuitously, took me close to Ximena and Rafael's house. I slowed down and turned off the major thoroughfare. Just as I started to accelerate again, I felt a tug from the engine of the car that didn't feel normal. I tried again, but there was no response from the car other than a deep, growling sound. I wasn't out of gas and hadn't had any problems with the car; I thought, "Oh *****. It's the transmission. I know it is." With nothing else to do, I pulled the car over to the side of the road, rolled up the windows, got out and locked the car. This was a semi-residential neighborhood and could be just as dangerous as walking around *el centro,* but I had no choice. I was two blocks from the Francos' house. If I could just get there, then I could call the school, and they would send somebody to help. Every passing car was a potential threat, in my mind, and I walked as fast as I could. Finally, out of breath, I arrived on their doorstep and knocked on the door. It never occurred to me that they would have a new maid who didn't know me who wouldn't let me in to use the phone. Both Rafael and Ximena, and the girls, were out, and I quickly lost all of my Spanish skills.

All the maid said was, "No, they're not home. You can't come in."

I tried to explain who I was and what had happened, but she didn't budge an inch. Finally I asked, in Spanish, if she would call Rafael and ask if it was okay for me to use the phone. Begrudgingly, she eventually called him and then gave permission for me to enter the house. Relieved, and glad to be close to a bathroom, I called the school and told Marty what had happened. He said he would send somebody immediately and not to worry.

Before the school person arrived, Xavier showed up, said Rafael had called and he had come to see if he could help. When the mechanic from school arrived, the two of them drove to the broken-down car. I waited with the maid. Before long Xavier came back and said it was definitely the transmission.

"Somebody will tow the car back to the school, and I'll take you home," he said. "Do you need to go anywhere else?"

"No, going home will be fine," I answered, as, once again, I acknowledged my debt to these dear friends.

My days with the car were over, but it was fun.

Jodie and Janet were not due back for another week, so I had plenty of time to work on my documents for the adoption. At this point I was mainly getting copies made and getting them notarized.

One night on TV I watched the American Music Awards, which were presented in the States in January, and were just now, seven months later, being shown on the local channel. We didn't see programs from the States often, so I was excited the reception was clear that night. I was immediately blown away by Michael Jackson's energy, songs, and videos. The speeches were dubbed in Spanish, but not the music, and I couldn't believe the little brother from the Jackson Five had such remarkable talent. Lionel Richie, who hosted the show, was popular in Colombia and I was familiar with his music but not Michael Jackson. I was becoming more and more aware of how quickly I was losing touch with what was going on back home, and I didn't like the feeling.

Janet returned a couple of days early, and then Jodie moved in with her two roommates while they were looking for a house. For a week, the five of us shared the apartment, including two bathrooms, but, miraculously, got along fine with a schedule that accommodated all of us. When they soon found a place, our apartment emptied out again and we got back to normal.

Excited about being in Cali, the new teachers arrived and settled in quickly. At school-sponsored get-togethers, I met all of them and thought they were a lively and friendly group. They were eager to get started.

Finally, during the last week of August, our students arrived, and we, the teachers, anticipated a productive year. Starting a new school year is like being given a second chance to start a project all over again. It's an opportunity to put to work lessons learned previously, meet new people, learn new skills, and grow as an individual. I was ready to get started because I knew I had some big changes coming.

September 1984

The rainy season moved in on schedule, and at times the deluges caused flooding. Pictures in the newspaper showed people navigating the streets in boats, and cartoonists made jokes. The Cauca Valley, where Cali is, was declared a disaster area, and power outages caused a lot of disruptions. Many nights we lost power when our dinner was in the oven and we had to resort to makeshift meals. Shoes didn't last long in weather like that, and I was constantly on the lookout for new ones. Most of the rain, fortunately, came at night, so during the day we only had to hop the puddles.

At school when the electricity flickered, I could hear Russell, the computer coordinator, moaning when the computers went down and all was lost. There were some brave souls who developed the computer curriculum in 1984 while experimenting with the few computers at Colegio Bolivar, and I wondered how, and if, they would ever be able to move into the Age of Technology.

My new schedule included Geometry and Algebra II. I knew most of the students in Algebra since I had taught them the year before. Even though I had a heavier load than the previous semester, and the SAT class coming in October, it was still lighter than the class sizes I usually had in the States. Also, I had plenty of time to finish my preparation and grading at school, and I didn't feel over-extended. The students, too, were friendly, respectful, and fun to be around.

Soon after the beginning of school, Marty called me to his office again. He quickly got to the point.

"Patricia, I noticed your application says you've had experience on SACS committees during accreditation. We're starting our two-year self-study evaluation, and I hope you will chair the Math committee. We need somebody with experience, and I think you'd be just the right person."

I had been on many self-study committees and chaired a lot of them, but they were always for a high school, not K-12. When I mentioned this, Marty assured me that past studies and resources were available, and he didn't seem to think I would have a problem.

"Also, Marty, you know that I'm right in the middle of adopting a child, and there's still a lot of uncertainty about what's going to happen. If the adoption happens soon, and I'm able to get the child's visa for the States, then I'll probably be leaving next summer. My schedule is up in the air. It would be hard to commit to anything beyond one more year, at this point," I said.

"Patricia," he answered, "we are accustomed to dealing with uncertainty here. If you'd be willing to take on this job, then, we can work with you as your plans become more concrete. If you end up staying for just one year, then we can handle that. For us, what we need right now is someone with your expertise to get the program off the ground. And I may have forgotten to mention that there will be a stipend, because we know there's a lot of extra work involved. Would you be interested in giving it a try?"

With an offer like that, I had to say yes and took on the new responsibilities with enthusiasm. It was a professional opportunity that I was eager to embrace, and I immediately started rounding up materials, organizing meetings and planning strategies. I felt as if I was right on track.

Toward the end of September, with all going well, I received a call at school from Chiquitines. Elsa, one of the secretaries in the high school office, rushed down to my room and said that Bienestar would like to interview me the next day. Could I meet them at the orphanage at 3:00 p.m.?

"Elsa, tell them I'll be there," I said. My last class ended at 2:15, and the Blanco y Negro bus went right by there. By the time I left school that day, several people had heard about my appointment and shared their support and excitement.

Getting through the first interview with Bienestar, the Colombian Welfare Department, was an important step in securing my approval for adoption. I had no idea what would be involved, but my instincts told me to be as honest as possible. They were the experts, and trying to present myself in any way other than completely straightforward, would not pass muster. I knew they would ask a lot of personal questions at this meeting.

When I arrived at Chiquitines, Sra. Carvajal met me and introduced me to Sra. Echeverry, a licensed Social Worker.

"Patricia, I'm very glad to meet you. Sra. Carvajal sent me your papers, and what you have turned in is complete. We now have to do the social study, and the first part is our interview today. Later, I will come to your home, and we will talk again. After that, when you have spent time with the child, we will meet again before the child actually moves in." She was formal, polite and professional.

Sra, Echeverry knew a lot about me, and today we talked about my own family and my life as a child. She asked about my relationship with parents and siblings when I was growing up, and now. She also wanted to know about my marriage and subsequent divorce. There was no way I could avoid that discussion, and I was as honest and forthright as possible. We soon moved on to other topics. Did I plan to stay in Colombia after the adoption? How did my roommate Janet feel about a child moving in our apartment? What about school for the child?

Throughout the interview I was aware that her main concern was for the well-being and protection of the child. She was fair and upfront, and she treated me with respect. We talked for about an hour, and, as I was leaving, she said with a kind smile, "Be patient, these things take time, but it's because we want to do the right thing for the child."

"Thank you, Sra. Echeverry, I understand," I said, as we shook hands. I couldn't remember ever talking that much about myself and hoped I hadn't said too much.

October 1984

Nearly every week, more items were disappearing from shelves in the grocery stores. Aluminum foil, which I had been happy to find in Cali, was one of the first things to go. The diet drink "Tab" and popcorn were soon gone, along with raisins. Local foods were becoming more expensive, and chicken became a luxury item. The Chilean wines, which had been affordable, were now for special occasions only, and even cheese was too expensive for most of us. There were still, however, plenty of potatoes, rice, beef, and local fruits. These shortages were supposedly due to President Betancur's austerity program, but we all had our doubts. We thought the disappearance of the imported US products might somehow be connected to the growing anti-American sentiments.

As the new teachers settled in, they were sharing the Friday night hostessing duties. Dan T., the high school principal, and Russell, the computer coordinator, entertained the new teachers and the other import teachers at their lovely home on the outskirts of town. Cali was always an ideal setting for outdoor get-togethers, and we ate a delicious meal of grilled beef and potluck dishes the rest of us brought. We sat outside in chairs and held our plates in our laps or sat in the grass.

Lynn, a new teacher from California, had come to Cali with her two high school-aged sons. She bought a car as soon as she arrived, found a house, and was exploring the city in no time. She and I became great friends.

Jeff B. and Lynnett, young Science teachers, decided to rent a house together after meeting during the orientation. They were both active in Sports and were experimenting with recycling in their kitchen.

Jeff S., a widower with two young children, was a tall, lanky, friendly guy who participated in all the activities and had everyone's admiration. The single women teachers gave him more than a second glance.

Nancy was returning to Colegio Bolivar for her second assignment. She had previously taught there for two years, returned to her home in the States for a while, and then decided that Cali was where she wanted to be. Her command of Spanish was exceptional.

Mark and Phyllis were a young married couple with ties to Nicaragua.

Mike and Linda were from Arizona, and Linda was of Mexican heritage.

Over the course of the year, I had a chance to know them all. My friends from the previous semester, Jodie, Janet, David, and Dan W. were there, and my range of friends was wide. With my Colombian friends also, I always had something to do if I had time. Whenever someone from school had a party, we all were compatible—a mixture of import and local teachers, along with a few children.

Already familiar with the city, I was selective in choosing when to go out. The new teachers explored the local culture as I focused on the upcoming adoption and extra work at school. I was happy to represent the school at an outdoor cocktail party for a group of college representatives from the States who were touring private schools in South America. This kind of activity was more in line with my life at this time.

The mother of one of my students worked at *La Tertulia,* the modern-art museum in Cali, and often sent me tickets to opening nights. Since she always provided two tickets, I usually invited another teacher to go with me. Lynn from California was an Arts enthusiast, so she would travel downtown to the museum with me. When a show opened for Canadian artists, Lynn and I met the Canadian Consul, who charmed us with his French-accented English.

In early October the school planned a weekend trip for teachers to the *Grajales*, the wine-making region in Colombia. They promised us a weekend of good food, swimming, and relaxation. The wine had a reputation of being so bad that I decided not to go, and the trip was eventually canceled for lack of interest.

In regular letters from home, Mother reported that the school system in Florence, S.C., close to Whiteville, had hired Math teachers from Germany because of the shortage of qualified personnel. She didn't want me to forget that I needed to return to the States. She also sent me the biography of Margaret Mitchell, author of *Gone With the Wind*, which I couldn't put down. Soon after that I found an old, dog-eared copy of *GWTW* in our school library and took it home to read. I was probably the only Southerner over the age of twelve who had never read it and, again, I couldn't put it down.

A couple of weeks before the SAT class was scheduled to start, Marty called me to his office again. He wanted to enroll the seventh-grade students in an experimental program for gifted/ talented students. A testing service in the States wanted to identify top scoring private schools in Colombia. To prepare them for the SAT, I would teach test-taking skills and also cram as much secondary math into them as possible. It would meet after school two days a week and would pay an additional stipend. I agreed to do it.

"Okay, Marty, that will be four afternoons a week for six weeks. Still not as much time as 'South Pacific,' so how can I say no?" Besides, I was concerned about money.

The SAT classes were a huge success. Scores were high, and Marty was already talking about repeating the classes second semester for other grade levels. The parents of the seventh-grade students were thrilled, and I was gratified. I reminded Marty and the others that excellent teachers had prepared these students before the prep class. It was my good fortune to guide them through the last preparation, and I felt honored. Before the fall semester ended, Marty talked about plans for the spring semester and beyond, and my involvement in the overall plan. We agreed to talk in more detail after exams.

One Sunday afternoon when I was trying to nap, I woke up to the sound of horse's hooves. I felt sure the Indians weren't passing through town because they moved during the night, and I finally got up to see what was happening. When I looked out the living room window, I saw a horse parade passing down Roosevelt with vaqueros carrying banners and signs in support of cancer research. Men (I didn't see any women) wore leather chaps or black pants, with white shirts, boleros, and red scarves. Most were wearing black cowboy hats. The horses were also decked out in their finery, and from eight floors up I saw a lot of silver. Some of the horses were prancing like Tennessee Walkers, and then there were mules just loping along. I could hear music but had no idea where it was coming from. All were proudly participating, and I was glad to see support for a cause that knows no cultural or international boundaries. Living on a main street of Cali was always full of surprises, and I gladly relinquished the nap for the spectacle of the parade.

Near the end of October, Sra. Carvajal called the school and asked if I could come by the orphanage the next day to meet some of the children. She also said I could take a friend with me if I wanted. I took that as a positive sign and immediately asked Ximena. We met there the next afternoon.

"Patricia, we have identified a few children we think might be good matches for you. Why don't you and Ximena visit with them today and then go home and think about them. I have information on all of them and will answer your questions at our next meeting," she said. "It's good that you brought Ximena because the children speak no English and Ximena can help, if needed. They're in the play room now."

"Thank you, Sra. Do they know they're being considered for adoption? Are they old enough to understand what's going on?" I asked.

"Yes, to both questions. With their limited experience they are aware they could possibly be moving to a new home. They're all in the process of being declared legally available for adoption, and that includes visiting a psychiatrist on a regular basis. As I said, I can tell you more about them individually later. Today, you can get to know them."

With that, Ximena and I went to the room where several children were playing games, running around, and chatting with each other. Crayons and drawing paper were on the tables, and the late afternoon sun was turning a golden color. An adult showed us where we could sit and talk to the children.

She introduced one little girl and two little boys, five or six years old. Elisa was a pretty little girl with long, ash blond hair and a pale face full of freckles. With a coy smile and flirtatious manner, she snuggled up to us quickly. Paco was darker, with a head full of straight, coal black hair and huge black eyes. He had a sad grin and tilted his head to one side as we talked to him. James had thin, wispy brown hair, a distended stomach and was the smallest of the group. Not shy at all, he spoke to me as if I understood everything he was saying. Even if Ximena had not been with me, we could have communicated. We talked about what games they were playing, what they liked to do.

We all walked outside to the playground area where Ximena and I pushed them on swings. Laughing and enjoying the attention, they latched onto us quickly. As they played, I looked at each individually and tried to imagine one as my own child. This had to be the most difficult part of adopting: choosing one from among several. I could easily conceive of taking each one of them home, and I hoped that when the time came to decide that I would have divine guidance. The children seemed sad when we had to leave, and I wondered how I would ever be able to select just one of them.

Ximena and I said our goodbyes to the children and the adults. Sra. Carvajal told me, away from the children, to call her in a week, and we could make an appointment to discuss the children individually. I felt as if I had just seen my first sonogram.

"Patricia," Ximena said. "That little boy James, did you hear him ask if you were going to be his mother? I'm pretty sure he's the one who asked that the first time we were here."

"No, I didn't hear him. This is almost overwhelming. How am I ever going to select just one of those children?" I answered.

"I think this is why Sra. Carvajal asked you to wait a week before coming back. She knows it's going to take some time. And don't forget, you don't have to make up your mind immediately. What you need to do now is give it time to soak in and then spend some time with each one individually. Eventually, you'll know which one."

I had no choice but to believe what Ximena was telling me. With her unsentimental assessment, she gave me the strength I needed.

November 1984

On November 6, election day in the States, The American Men's Society of Cali hosted a cocktail party for North American citizens at the Intercontinental Hotel. The election was big news even though Mondale was an unlikely candidate, and there were no surprises when results started coming in on a short wave radio. Reagan was viewed as the best choice, even though many disagreed with his nuclear arms policy. Always curious about stateside politics, the Colombians listened to the outcome of the race as closely as we U.S. citizens did. Their big concern was whether (or when) Reagan was going to invade Nicaragua. But the biggest news in Colombia was the "Miss Colombia" beauty pageant in Cartagena. Always scheduled to coincide with Colombian Independence Day celebrations (November 11), it creates more excitement than national elections. The schools in Cartagena have a vacation during that week, and the newspapers and TVs give the glamorous festivities full coverage.

M-19, the urban guerilla group, was also in the news nearly every day as opposition to the United States' involvement in Central and South America increased. The guerillas used the US election coverage to criticize the U.S. extradition treaty and promised more violence if drug lords were returned to the States for trial. We were all on alert.

Robberies, while not directly connected to guerilla activity, touched several of us during this time. Two of the male teachers at school were robbed at a Reggae concert. One lost his eyeglasses as well as forty dollars. The other also lost cash and his billfold. To make matters worse, the police carried out the crime, and as was typical, the teachers had no recourse.

Janet and I changed maids when we realized a child would, in all likelihood, be moving in and we would need live-in help. To be honest, we didn't check out her credentials as carefully as we should have, and the first day she was there she stole six hundred dollars in cash from Janet's bedroom and took all of my jewelry. She didn't find my cash, and my jewelry was not that valuable, but Janet, of course, was devastated. People told us to consider ourselves lucky that it wasn't worse and to accept our losses. We had become too complacent. Our next maid came with glowing references, and we checked her out thoroughly.

I discovered a group in Cali that showed foreign and independent films, which I was fond of, on Saturday mornings. They showed old movies, usually classics, as well as new ones. The first one I saw was the original "Moulin Rouge," the story of Toulouse-Lautrec's life, starring Jose Ferrer. Dan W. also liked these movies and went with me to the second one I saw, "Bolero," by Claude LeLouch, a French director, and many others. We followed up these trips to the cinema with shopping and sightseeing trips. Usually, we stopped by Esteban's restaurant, Northside Pizzeria, for a late lunch and visited with any family members there.

A week after I visited Chiquitines I called Sra. Carvajal and asked if I could take James out on Saturday. I had found myself thinking of him more than the others and decided to have my first outing with him. We would go to the school where we could swim in the pool, have a picnic, and then return in the afternoon. It would be just the two of us. With a lilt in her voice, she said that he would be ready at 10:00 a.m.

On Saturday morning, with a picnic packed, towels and bathing suit in my backpack, a first-aid kit, suntan lotion and a camera all in tow, I took the public bus to the orphanage. Sra. Carvajal and a shy, grinning James met me at the gate. After a few pleasantries, James and I were off. Someone had packed a little bathing suit for him in a plastic grocery bag. We took the Blanco y Negro bus to the school since it was more comfortable and would not involve changing buses.

During the forty-minute trip, James looked out the window, smiling, laughing, and chattering. He may never have been on a bus before. At one point, after he had settled down, I noticed out of the corner of my eye that he was staring at me. He was as curious about me as I was about him. We sat together comfortably for the duration of the trip, and when we got to our stop, James jumped out ahead of me and down the bus steps. The next time, I thought, I should get off first.

To get to the school grounds, we had to go through the security gate. The guards knew me, and when I introduced James to them, they made a big fuss over him, told him to have a good time and be careful in the pool, all in Spanish. We walked down the sloping path across the campus to the gym where we changed clothes and used the bathrooms. James was bouncing. I showed him where the showers were and then pointed out the water fountain which he immediately tried out. There was a small one for the little kids at school, and he seemed to think it was a great toy. James cupped water in his hands and tossed it around the room before I could explain that the water was for drinking. Once we finished exploring the gym, we went to the pool where I spread out our towels and got ready for a good swim. I applied suntan lotion to both of us, and James thought that was hilarious.

The Olympic-size pool had a shallow end about three feet deep. James was not much taller, so we carefully walked down the steps into the water, holding hands. I could tell he was uncomfortable and realized that he couldn't swim. I squatted down in the water, and James grabbed onto my shoulders like a little monkey. We waded back and forth in the water for a while, and gradually he relaxed a little. I tried to get him to stretch out his legs and practice kicking, but that seemed to frighten him. At the edge of the pool, I showed him how to hold on to the side and practice kicking. This was easier, and eventually James let me support him while he kicked. I couldn't remember how I had learned to swim. So, I took my cues from him and let him hold onto me as long as he needed. We played and laughed in the water, and after the first swimming lesson, we got out, dried off, and sat down for lunch.

Curious about lunch, James looked at everything carefully and then started on his sandwich, which was ham, cheese, lettuce and tomato on whole-wheat bread. He ate all of that, then ate a small bag of chips, then a banana, and then a cookie. Then he drank his juice. Each one, individually, until it was gone. It seemed like a lot of food for such a little kid, but I was glad he had enjoyed it and just hoped he wouldn't get sick from eating too much. We cleaned up everything when we finished and then returned to the gym to use the bathrooms. We decided to take one more dip in the pool before leaving and walked down the steps together, again, as we held on to each other. He was a natural in the water, and it wouldn't take him long to learn to swim. And he was a cutie, to boot.

On the ride back to Chiquitines, I was feeling so encouraged that I was already thinking about our next Saturday together. Today was just one day, but it had been fulfilling, and I knew I was on the right track. When we parted ways that afternoon, Sra. Carvajal asked how we had gotten along and if there had been any problems. I knew it was the honeymoon stage, but my instincts about this little boy were strong, and I knew I wanted to know him better.

The next Saturday, we did the same thing, but went to the Club instead, where several people from school were also spending the day. They joked around with James, he played soccer with some of the other children (he was a natural at that, too) and practiced his swimming, while holding on to me. After leaving the Club, we walked to the mall and ate ice cream cones before going back to the orphanage. When we were walking together, he tended to walk behind me if I wasn't holding his hand. Someone told me he did that so he could see me better, so I had to adjust our way of walking together, so I could see him, too.

When we returned to Chiquitines, Sra. Carvajal said that the paperwork was progressing to allow me to adopt James, if he was the one I wanted to adopt. We made plans to spend more time together after the upcoming holidays, and she asked if I wanted to spend time with any of the other children. In a split-second decision I told her I was comfortable with James and would very much like to pursue his adoption. She smiled and said, "I thought you felt that way."

Thanksgiving was approaching, and since Colegio Bolivar, just like Colegio Nueva Granada, recognized stateside holidays, we were also making plans for our celebration. Jeff S. volunteered to host the party which was scheduled at 6:30 p.m. on the Wednesday before Thanksgiving. At school, Thursday was a half day for students, and teachers were scheduled to take part in curriculum workshops until 3:00 p.m. when a group of us would then leave on an eight-hour bus trip to Pasto.

Marty had found a turkey somewhere and cooked it at his house before arriving at Jeff's. Jose Luis from Argentina was cooking beef over an open grill. Aromas of garlic, cilantro, onions, potatoes, and platanos mixed with sage, cinnamon, and brown sugar. Everybody else brought potluck dishes, and when I arrived with Dan W. and Nancy, a big crowd had already gathered. Salsa music was blaring, people were milling around the yard and patio area, and tables were filling up with delectable looking food. Hopefully, the rainy season had ended, and the sun was still visible as we settled in for another celebration of our North American heritage.

It was November 21, and we, the females, were wearing sleeveless blouses, shorts or capris, and sandals. Most of the guys were wearing sandals, too, but a few were wearing sneakers. A lot of men were also wearing shorts and sleeveless t-shirts. Sweaters and wraps were in our bags, though, since the nights cooled down quickly. I smiled when I thought about the white shoes we wore year-round here in Cali, and the fact that it was well past Labor Day. I remembered Thanksgiving in 1975, when a group of import teachers hovered around a fire in Bogotá, high in the Andes, staying warm with our wool socks and ruanas as the unrelenting rain soaked the city. But the thing I thought about most that day, in addition to the fallen leaves and explosion of color in the trees back home, was the possibility that next Thanksgiving, I could have a son. For me, it was an astonishing possibility.

The Thanksgiving dinner was another great celebration and, because we still had a half-day of school on Thursday, we finished early and went home to pack for our trip to Pasto.

Most of us had not been on a good trip in several weeks, so when the school organized a visit to Pasto, we jumped at the chance. Located in the southern part of Colombia, about fifty miles from the Ecuadorian border, Pasto sits on a plateau high on the Andes cordillera. At an altitude of 8,291 ft., nearly as high as Bogotá, the climate is much cooler, especially at night, because the city is farther from the Equator.

About twenty of us, teachers, office staff, children and some spouses, left school at 3 p.m. on Thursday for an eight-hour ride through the mountains. The bus reminded me of old activity buses back in the States that sports teams and bands rode to away games. In other words - hard seats, no bathrooms on board, and very little leg room. Everybody was in a good frame of mind when we left, though, and we did not begrudge a little discomfort for such a promising trip. For a couple of hours, we talked and marveled at the changing scenery as we left our own Cauca Valley. The topography quickly became sharper as mountains grew and bottomless ravines suddenly appeared. The bus would slow down so much on ascents that we felt like we could walk faster and then, all of a sudden, plunge into what we thought was surely sudden death. Soon, the terrifying ordeal eased up, and we were happy to reach our first stop, an outdoor restaurant frequented by travelers.

The bathrooms were adequate, the food was comforting, and we had a chance to stretch our legs. We pulled out sweaters and jackets before getting back on the bus, and everybody switched seats. From that point on, we stopped every two hours and switched seats. The guys who were tall were really suffering from being so cramped, and at some point, Jeff S, probably about 6'5", got out of his seat and stretched out on the floor using his backpack as a pillow. Soon, a couple of others followed suit until all the space down the center of the bus was filled. That freed up more space in the seats for the rest of us, so we started taking turns having a full seat to ourselves for a while.

Tired, cramped and cold, we finally arrived at a pension in Pasto near midnight where we would spend one night before going to the much-touted chalet the next day. This was a true pension, a backpacker's dream, and it was probably a good choice for that first night because we were so tired all we wanted to do was stretch out and sleep: it didn't much matter where. Who cared if we had to walk down the hall to a bathroom shared with numerous strangers? Not I, for sure.

The pension was located on a side street of the small city right across from a *panadería* famous for its *pan de bono,* my favorite Colombian indulgence. So, as soon as we were up and moving the next day, we invaded the little shop and had our fill along with *café con leche.* Before going to the chalet, we rode on the bus to a toy factory famous for colorful handmade dolls. The guides were friendly and eager to show us how the dolls were made. There were many handicrafts made of wood, leather, and wool. On the way, we also saw dairy farms and furniture factories, both vital to the local economy.

When we finally arrived at the chalet, although it was only lunch time, most of us were still tired from the long, uncomfortable trip the day before and the sagging, primitive beds at the pension. The breathtaking view of the chalet and surrounding area, however, rejuvenated all of us. The chalet belonged to a German family that had moved to Colombia in the late 1930s, probably as close to a replica of their homeland as anywhere. Self-sustaining, the farm provided everything needed by the owners and their guests.

We walked into a lodge with a huge fireplace and blazing fire. Comfortable couches and chairs, tables for eating meals or playing games, bookcases filled with books in many languages, and a spectacular view of the mountains were more than we could have hoped for. Upon arrival and before lunch, the owners offered the adults hot-buttered rum and the children hot chocolate. We gratefully accepted and sat down by the fire to sip our drinks and thaw out from the bus with no heat.

The late lunch was our main meal that day, and we dined on rabbit in wine sauce. I had never eaten rabbit before and found it surprisingly delectable. The savory sauce was creamy and smooth and flavorful. The salad and potatoes, also from the farm, were just as good.

After lunch we rested in our rooms. Nancy and I were sharing a room, and the first things we noticed were pipes running around the perimeter of the ceiling. We thought it must be steam heat and hoped so because we were freezing. Hissing sounds of water coursed through the pipes, and we were relieved because, even though we were cold then, we had heard about below freezing temperatures at night.

We spent two nights in that bucolic setting. During the day, we sat in the lodge by the fire, played card games, read, and talked. Jeff's daughter, who was eight years old, sat with us, and we plaited her hair one morning and painted her fingernails. A couple of the young boys played in the yard with the resident Labrador Retriever. We walked around the farm and took pictures. Our main meal the next day was fresh mountain trout, and it was exquisite. Our breakfasts were eggs and fried platanos with *café con leche* or *tinto*.

After two days, we called on all the resolve we had and packed our backpacks for the trip home. Nobody wanted to think about the hard seats on that bus through the mountains, but by the time we got back to Cali, everybody was glad we had persevered. About an hour before arriving at the school, the mood picked up, people were laughing and talking, and the bus ride would soon become a memory to smile about. The trip to Pasto was one of the highlights of my time in Colombia.

December 1984

"Yanqui goes home!" "Yanqui get out of Central America and South America!" These were the messages the M-19 group painted around town on buildings and yelled during their rallies. Marty quickly organized a meeting to review security measures in case an evacuation was necessary. Missionaries whose children attended our school were contacted by the American Embassy in Bogotá and told to be prepared to leave quickly on short notice. The growing involvement of the US in Panama and other parts of Central America was fueling a lot of unrest, even though the U.S. Government at times ignored Noriega's drug dealings and money-laundering schemes. The M-19 existed because of the drug trade, and so the U.S. was a real threat to them.

The Colombo-Americano, the cultural branch of the American Embassy, closed in Bogotá, but the one in Cali remained open. Security was extremely tight there, as it was in any place where groups of North Americans gathered. I was scheduled to take the GRE (Graduate Record Exam) there on December 8, and Marty said it would probably be canceled. Public buses became risky, so far, because of harassment, so we were encouraged to ride in private vehicles if possible. In the mornings, we were told to wait inside our apartment building until the school bus arrived and not to gather on the sidewalk.

Cabin fever sets in quickly under these circumstances, and we had to watch out for complacency and irritability. The school tried hard to keep us alert and aware. Amid all of the disruptions, the

Christmas season arrived. From our apartment, we could see the colored lights in the Mall and wondered about the brisk business. The annual fair in Cali was still on schedule for December 26 through January 4, complete with bullfights, beauty pageants, and salsa dancing.

I took the GRE at the Colombo-Americano with no problems other than having to be there from 8:00 a.m. until 5:30 p.m. Marty had advised me to take my lunch since leaving the building and walking around the area could be dangerous, so I was actually inside the entire time. Other than an official who administered the test and security guards outside, I was the only person there. Someone from school took me in the morning and picked me up in the afternoon.

Two weeks before Christmas holidays, Sra. Echeverry from the adoption agency scheduled a home visit. As part of the process, she also wanted to meet Janet and our maid, Esmeralda. Our apartment was spotless, thanks to Esmeralda, and all three of us were waiting. I had bought a bed for James's bedroom but was holding off buying more pieces until the adoption was confirmed.

Our guest was hot when she arrived, and when I offered her something to drink, she asked for yogurt. She knew that we were not permanent residents of Cali and would probably leave in another year or two. Therefore, she understood that we didn't have more than we needed in the apartment. After talking briefly to Janet and Esmeralda, they left and Sra. and I continued talking. I showed her around the apartment and pointed out the room where James would sleep and the bathroom that he and I would share. We walked downstairs to a green area where children in the complex played, and at that point, she said it would now be appropriate for James to come for an overnight stay.

Sra. Echeverry's visit lasted about forty-five minutes, and I felt encouraged when she left. I immediately called Sra. Carvajal at Chiquitines to arrange for James to stay with me the coming weekend. I wanted to make sure we could spend time together before the Christmas holidays, and fortunately the scheduling was convenient.

During the few days I had at school before James came for his first overnight visit, I told my friends about the event. They were happy and wanted to help. Since I had planned a trip to the Club for our Saturday activity, several said they would meet us there where we could swim, James could play soccer, and we could all relax. I was getting excited.

On Saturday morning, I took the bus again to Chiquitines where a rather nervous James was waiting with Sra. Carvajal. He was dressed in a cotton shirt and shorts and carried his bathing suit in a plastic bag. His thin hair was wet, and someone had parted it on the side and combed it back. As the three of us talked, Sra. Carvajal made sure James understood that he would be spending the night in our apartment and returning to the orphanage the next day. His eyes were bulging, and I couldn't tell if it was from excitement or fear. I took his hand, and we walked to the bus stop.

Ordinarily, the bus was not too crowded, but that day there was only one vacant seat. I took the seat and James sat on my lap and squirmed while I tried to hold onto him and my bags. I explained that we were going to the apartment first and then to the club. At the apartment, I introduced him to the security guards who were brandishing their firearms. When he saw them, James pointed and started howling as if he were terrified. I quickly tried to explain that the guards were not going to hurt us but were there to protect us. We entered the building, and I could only guess why he may have had that fear. Riding the elevator took his mind off the guards and their rifles, and he tried to punch all the buttons after he saw me press the 8. Fortunately, I caught him before any damage was done, and we rode all the way to the eighth floor without making any stops.

Esmeralda, Janet, and David were waiting for us, and they welcomed him profusely. Esmeralda offered him some juice, and soon he was lively and engaged again. Janet and David both practiced their Spanish with him and made him feel comfortable. After a quick tour of the apartment and a look at his bedroom and the bathroom, we got our things together and left for the club. I had anticipated that he would not have any clothes, so I had picked up a few basic items such as a toothbrush, a couple of t-shirts and shorts, underwear, and Spiderman pajamas. I planned to buy shoes as soon as I could get him to a store.

James was familiar with the club now and several of the other teachers and children. Still not swimming alone yet, he was making progress and was thrilled when Dan W. offered to go in the pool with him. I was hoping my men friends would be around because I knew he needed male role models. Plus, he was, at times, loud and boisterous and didn't always respond to my reprimands as well as he did to the men. He had trouble seeing me as an authority figure, which I chalked up to his limited experience with women, even as a street kid, in a macho society. All of that would change in time, but in the beginning, he was challenging, and the males in our group seemed to garner a certain respect that I didn't.

We spent a few hours at the club, and by the time we left, James was worn out. He had been in and out of the pool several times, played soccer, eaten enough to last a couple of days, so I was hoping he would go to bed early and sleep well. He did go to bed early, but sometime during the night he woke up crying. I ran to his room and found him cowering and shaking under the covers. We always slept with the windows open and didn't worry about anyone climbing through them, since we were on the eighth floor. But, apparently, the curtains, blowing in the wind in the dark, strange room, were just enough to fuel his imagination and scare him out of his wits. I closed the windows and pulled up a chair beside his bed. His tears soon stopped, and, holding onto my hand tightly, he went back to sleep. Before leaving his room, I moved the night light to a more visible spot.

Janet and I had a subscription to the newspaper and picked it up from the portero at the gate on the way to work. On the weekends, we usually picked it up and took it back to the apartment. On that Sunday morning, I woke up before James and decided to run down for the paper since Janet was away for the weekend. When I looked in James' room, he seemed to be sleeping soundly, and then I slipped out the door for no more than five minutes. He must have heard me leave because when I came back he was in the living room, crouched inside a cardboard box in the corner, sobbing. This time, I was the one who was terrified. When I found him and decided he was scared again but not hurt, I was relieved. I did everything I could to coax him out. I explained where I had been and tried to reassure him that he was not alone and that I would

193

never leave him. It took a lot of time to get him to leave the box, and when he finally came out, we sat on the couch, and he snuggled up while I tried to comfort him. The emotional outburst subsided, and I think he finally forgave me. That was the last time I ever left him alone without telling him where I was going.

We ate a big breakfast of scrambled eggs, pineapple, bread, and coffee for me. A lot of children in Colombia drank coffee but I was hesitant to give him any just yet, and he didn't ask for it. I showed him how to use the shower and, again, demonstrated how to brush his teeth. In a much better mood, he was ready for our trip to the river with Esteban, Marta, and Isa.

They were delighted to meet him and treated him like a very special guest. Esteban insisted that James ride in the front seat of the car with him while Marta, Isa, and I sat in the back. Of course, they were all speaking Spanish to him and that, in itself, seemed to give him confidence. We had a great day on the river, and before returning home we stopped at Esteban's restaurant, Northside Pizzeria, for James' first pizza. He was gobbling it up so fast, Esteban finally said, *"Despacio, James, tómate tu tiempo."* "Slowly, James, take your time." He couldn't have been too hungry because we had been eating all day, but there was something in that pizza that he couldn't get enough of.

When we dropped him off at the orphanage around 5:00 p.m., Sra. Carvajal was waiting for him. She told me to call her the next day. We'd had a fun day together with the Platas, and I felt I was well on the way to getting to know this little seven-year-old boy. I was also very grateful to my friends for including us in their family trip.

James and I had two more visits before the holidays, and on the next trip, Sra. Carvajal told me what the orphanage knew about his background.

"Patricia, as you know, Colombian adoption laws are very clear. Before a child can be considered for adoption, he must be legally declared abandoned. James was taken to the 5th Police Station on May 28th, 1984 after some minors who were playing soccer in the street turned him in to a policewoman. He was called "James," and no other data was supplied. He was brought to us here, at Chiquitines, on that day. We posted an announcement on June 8th and July 3rd in the two local newspapers, along with his picture, and no one came to claim him. On August 13th, our appeal to declare him abandoned was accepted. On September 5th, a legal medical examination registered his birth as September 17th, 1977. His name was James Gonzales. The official report was filed with the Judicial Office in Bogotá on October 12th, so you are now free to continue with the adoption request."

"So nothing else is known about his past?" I asked.

"There is information about his mother, who lived on the street, and the possibility that his father may have been North American. That's not definite. Most of these street children are actually abandoned long before they come to Chiquitines and have had to survive any way they could. Probably the only stability he's had in his life came from being here these last few months. We think that with love and attention he'll be able to adjust and function like any other child. He seems to be happy with you." Sra. Carvajal then handed me a list of other steps I needed to take.

"I don't anticipate that there will be any problems with the adoption. Practically everything has been done and probably, soon after Christmas, he can move in with you permanently. It may take a couple of months to get the final adoption papers, due to the backlog in the courts, but it won't be necessary to wait until then for him to move in. The only thing you need to be aware of is the amount of time it could take to get his Visa to enter the States. Sometimes that can be the most difficult part of the adoption process. And you can't apply for that until you have the final adoption decree."

She had been through this process many times, and I hung onto her every word. Visa. That was the word I kept hearing and wondered how it could be so difficult for an American citizen to get that card for their legally adopted child. It was mid-December 1984, and surely, I thought, everything will be in order for us to return together to the States by July 1985.

With the adoption a near certainty, I was looking forward to sharing the news with my family. In addition to the excitement and anticipation, I constantly felt annoyed with the need to be so vigilant in the city and decided to go home to North Carolina for the Christmas holidays. That was a good move because, even though I didn't tell all of my friends or even family about the adoption, I was able to check on my condominium, inquire about jobs, and pick up some clothes and a few books and toys for James. Being there was an opportunity to relax and recharge, and I took full advantage of it.

After a couple of weeks, feeling those stirrings of nostalgia, I was on my way back to Colombia and ready for the final push to secure my son's Visa. Without that, any plans I might make would fall by the wayside, so I had been cautious about any commitments for housing or jobs, in Cali or in the States.

January 1985

On January 6, 1985, my forty-first birthday, I returned to Cali on the same day that four Colombians were extradited to the United States for drug trafficking. President Betancur called the bluff of the Mafioso, who had threatened terrorist activities if Colombians were extradited, and the citizens were cheering. There was no immediate repercussion from FARC or M-19, but an active period of bombings, kidnappings and violence was just beginning.

At school, we were two weeks away from exams, so we jumped right in with reviews, phone calls, and parent conferences. As lively and delightful as my students were, when it came time for evaluations, they were dead serious. So, teaching was a joy, even in the uncertain political environment surrounding our school.

High on my agenda at school was a decision involving my plans for the next year. Marty always talked to the import teachers individually in January and asked for a decision by February when he would attend recruiting fairs in the States.

I was extremely undecided about my plans. On one hand, I felt that it was of the utmost importance to get James to the States and enrolled in school there where he would be exposed to English. Even though he would soon be enrolled at Colegio Bolivar, where he would be studying English, I felt that he would benefit more from a total immersion in the States as soon as possible. Also, I was well aware of the need to begin contributing again to the North Carolina State Employees retirement and health care system and to include him on my policy. I wanted my family and friends in the

States to be a part of his life. The condominium, although rented, was not completely paying for itself either. After a year and a half, I needed a dollar salary. So, all of these forces were pulling on me.

Marty and I had an open and honest relationship, and I looked forward to talking to him. His unique perspective and experience had garnered my respect, and I listened carefully to what he said. He knew my concerns were based on my desire to provide the best situation possible for James.

"Patricia, it's been hard for us here to develop the Math program in the way we'd like to because of the inherent nature of our school. We have a high faculty turnover because most import teachers come for just two years, so, coupled with the lack of resource people, that means the program has improved very little. The Board and I would like to offer you a job for next year as part-time curriculum director and part-time gifted/talented teacher." He looked at me quizzically, with a grin. "Interested?"

"Of course," I replied, "I'm very interested."

"There would be the normal cost-of-living increase plus a dollar increase of $3,000 to $4,000. After the board meets in February, they'll let me know for sure. Also, there could be an increase in your housing subsidy plus other benefits if you're willing to stay. As far as the curriculum development, you'd have free rein to do whatever you want. Believe me, everything you might need would be available. And, your son's health insurance would be included on your policy."

"Marty, you know how I'm struggling with this decision. Everything you have offered is so tempting, but there's that one pull from home that I can't let go of. How soon do I need to let you know?" I asked.

"By the middle of February, at the latest. Take your time. But I do want to remind you of one important fact regarding the adoption. Remember the talk we had earlier about the adoptions taking longer than expected?" I nodded my head. "Well, the Visa can often take even longer. Visa requests from here go through U.S. Immigration Services in Panama, and you know that Noriega and the United States are barely coexisting now. There's talk of a military coup there, and if that happens, the U.S. Embassy could close, permanently or temporarily, and it could be months, or years, before all the backed-up paperwork is sorted through. I don't mean to alarm you, but you need to think about it before you make your decision."

I had vaguely thought about it, but things were going so well, or so I thought, that I never considered basing my decision on what was going on in Panama.

"Okay, Marty. Thank you. I am honored and flattered that you have made me this offer. That would be a dream job for me, and I will give it every consideration."

About a week after that meeting, I received the following letter from Dan T., my principal:

January 17, 1985

Dear Patricia,

Although I have not done a formal observation of teaching this school year, I feel that mid-year presents a logical point for offering an overall, and by definition, general assessment of your work.

In a phrase, I am highly satisfied with what you have given the students and the school as a whole. I am not usually one to hand out compliments, but I do feel that there is much that should have and could have been said earlier on to give you a notion of your fine contributions in a very consistent manner.

The students respect your knowledge of the subject matter and the very essential awareness that you have of their possibilities and limitations. By any standard that makes for a productive atmosphere in the classroom, something that is often a stranger to the field of mathematics. Besides this, your experience in curriculum lends an air of professionalism to the program that we have too seldom been blessed with. You are very aware of the global perspective and the rather special mix of factors that make this school what it is and what it can be.

All of this adds up to a job very, very well done and appreciated.

Sincerely,
Dan

Talk about a tough decision! Support and respect from the administration is important to any teacher, and to have such confidence in me expressed in such a positive way made a deep impression. There was still time to decide, and I was beginning to look for divine guidance.

By now, James was staying in the apartment on the weekends. My Colombian friends and colleagues from school involved us in their activities, and James seemed to be adjusting well. Finally, Sra. Carvajal said that he could move in permanently on January 26, and I made plans at school to enroll him in the kinder-5 class.

On January 25, I received a call from Chiquitines that Chicken Pox was making the rounds at the orphanage and that James had developed a fever and had broken out in blisters. It would be two weeks before he could leave. Disappointed, but aware of the need to be cautious, I waited to see if I had become infected as well, since we had spent so much time together recently. And sure enough, I came down with a mild case of Chicken Pox, which kept me out of school for a week. I made it back to school in time for final exams and was glad we both had that behind us.

During this turbulent and sometimes violent time, the news from the States, that the Colombians were interested in, concerned President Reagan's inauguration and Nancy Reagan's elegant wardrobe. Our families and friends back home called with concern when they heard about the demonstrations and bombings. My uncle Harry in Myrtle Beach called and encouraged me to leave. He had heard a report that hundreds of North Americans had left Colombia in January, mainly Embassy personnel, and he thought I should leave, too. Apparently, the news there was more threatening than what we were hearing, but then again, we didn't hear the same things. The big news in Colombia at the end of January was that Colombia had lost the soccer championship to Peru.

February 1985

Ximena and Rafael picked me up early on Saturday morning, February 9, for the long-awaited final trip to Chiquitines. Clean, nervous, and holding on to his little bag, James was waiting for us in the living room. He gave me a hesitant smile and hug. He, Ximena, Rafael, Sra. Carvajal, and I sat in the cramped office and discussed what would happen next with the adoption. Everything at this point was hinging on the attorney's ability to process the legal documents. Once that was done, Sra. Carvajal would help with the Visa and passport. We planned to talk later. Our visit was upbeat and optimistic, and when we left, James seemed happy. I tried to imagine what might be going through his little mind and knew that he was bravely entering a world he could not even imagine.

Ximena and I had planned earlier to drop off James and me at the apartment, and then she and Rafael would leave. She and Nora, her mother, thought it important that the two of us spend this special day together, while the bonding process was unfolding.

Once we were in the apartment, the first order of business was to change his clothes. I took the ill-fitting shorts and shirt he was wearing and placed them in a bag to return to the orphanage. As soon as we could get some new shoes, I was going to return the old shoes as well. Already familiar with the apartment, he went to the bathroom, looked in his room, and asked about Esmeralda, the maid. She ordinarily didn't work on the weekends but was coming in on Sunday afternoon to help him prepare for school. When we had unpacked, we walked over to the mall to buy the shoes.

I'm sure James had never had a new pair of shoes. He was wearing sandals that many other children had probably worn, and they were too big. When he walked, he slapped his feet down, and I don't know what would have happened if he'd tried to run. We found a children's store with sneakers and started looking at the different styles. He was more interested in the color than anything and ended up choosing white ones with a red stripe. After being properly fitted, and with a grin that stretched across his entire face, he lifted his arms as if he were going to fly and gingerly took his first steps. I regretted not having a camera with me that day because he was walking like a little bird, tiptoeing in the water's edge. When he got his bearing and walked across the room a few times, he was ready to fly, he had wings! He bounced and jumped up and down and turned in circles. The salesman stared in disbelief as Jamie squealed and laughed and hugged me. I had never seen a happier child. He couldn't tell me enough how much he loved me, but I knew already if he didn't get what he wanted, he would be defiant. That day, he loved me.

James and I stopped for lunch, walked around a while longer, and returned to the apartment later in the afternoon. We pulled out some books and snuggled on the couch while I read a story to him. We looked at pictures of my family, and I told him their names and let him repeat them to me. I showed him where the crayons, paper, and a few toys and games were, and he was happy. It was so tempting to buy everything I could find, but I knew that would be overwhelming. So, I tried to keep things simple. He slept well and long that night.

On Sunday, Janet and David came back, and we all went to the club to swim and relax. We ran into friends there, and James played hard. He was still not swimming on his own, but he loved being in the water and would go in with anybody who was willing to have a little monkey ride on their backs. I thought about how much it meant to him *and* to me to have a place to fit in with people who cared for us. I secretly wondered what it would be like in the States, wherever I might decide to live and work, and realized that life there would be different for us. Should I consider that in my decision about next year? Especially since we were going through a period of adjustment ourselves.

When we arrived back at the apartment, it was time to plan for Monday, James' first day at Colegio Bolivar. I showed him his backpack and told him that Esmeralda would pack lunch for him. Although he didn't really need many supplies at that level, I gave him a pencil and paper and told him his teachers would give him more papers the next day. He was excited about riding the school bus, and since he had been to the pool there, he was familiar with the school grounds. His teachers knew he was coming, and I was sure they would make him feel welcome. We laid out his clothes, and when he went to bed, he was looking forward to his new adventure.

There were no problems on the bus the next day, and he was a happy trooper with his backpack and new shoes. Since my planning period was the first period, I spent extra time with him that morning, and when I left him to go to my classes, he was busy with activities and didn't notice I had left.

At the end of the first week, his teachers reported that he was adjusting well. He learned to write his name, and around this time "James" became "Jamie." I didn't realize in the beginning that I could have changed his name, and by the time it could have been done legally, we were well into the adoption process. I decided to keep James, since he already knew the name, and even though it was pronounced differently in Spanish, *"Hah-mez,"* I felt that avoiding unnecessary changes would be beneficial. So, he became James Claude Woodard, Claude after an uncle of mine, with an *apodo,* nickname, of Jamie. The Woodard was more out of respect for my dad than because it was also my name.

Many of the teachers gave me hand-me-down clothes and books, toys and games for Jamie. At the end of the month the faculty surprised me with a shower at school on a Friday morning, one of our staff-development days. Jodie, one of my roommates from the first semester, made a book out of different colored construction paper with pictures she had cut out from magazines and glued to the pages. They were all pictures of a young boy and young woman. Each page had the first lines of familiar songs, such as: *Reach out and touch somebody's hand..., Make this world a better place if you can..., When you wish upon a star..., A dream is a wish your heart makes..., You just call out my name..., It had to be you, wonderful you..., Love is in the air..., Bless the beasts and the children, give them shelter from the storm. Keep them safe, keep them warm...,* and several others. Inside the booklet was a copy of the invitation Jodie had sent to the faculty for the party. She had drawn an airplane flying to the States with the date, time, etc. of the celebration.

She and some of the other teachers had made brownies and cookies that we all gobbled up, with juice and cups of fresh coffee made by the maids in the school kitchen. In addition to the many items I had already received, there were still more clothes and toys. The final gift was a money tree, which I had never seen before. I was astonished at their generosity and found their outpouring of love and support overwhelming. That was a day I would never forget.

Friends and colleagues at Colegio Bolívar, Cali, 1985.

A group of twelve from the school continued celebrating that night with a ride through the city on a *chiva,* one of the old, open-air buses seen in tourist ads and movies. Yellow, red, and blue, almost psychedelic in design, with music blaring, and decorations of streamers and paper flowers, they garner a lot of attention from the public as they bounce around the streets of Cali. One half expects to see chickens or goats (*chivas*) on board as the tourists travel back in time on this outdated mode of transportation. Jamie and the other children had a terrific time, and so did the adults. We stopped for dinner at an outdoor restaurant where Colombian country music was playing and danced in the cool night air while waiting for our food. Everybody danced with Jamie, and I couldn't remember ever seeing a child so happy. By the time we got home that night, he was barely awake and I felt blessed.

James and I developed our school routine quickly. We caught the bus together in the mornings, and on Monday, Wednesday and Friday afternoons he left on the early bus at 2:00 p.m. with the other kinder students. Esmeralda met him at the bus stop and walked him to the apartment. On Tuesdays and Thursdays, he came to my room at 2:00 and stayed with me until we left at 3:30. Sometimes we had a quick swim before going home. At other times, we stopped at a new shopping center and went to a movie. It was a schedule that worked well, and if we needed to make changes, it was not a problem. He liked going to school, and even though he was a year older than the other students in his class, he fit in easily. Still small, he was catching up and gradually putting on weight. His hair started filling in, and after a couple of weeks in the apartment, his appetite diminished only slightly. He ate anything I put in front of him, and I was glad to find out that he didn't have much of a sweet tooth. On school nights we had dinner, then read or played games, he had his bath, and then the lights went out for him at 8:00 p.m. And then I took care of myself. We kept that schedule until the end of the school year, and he never complained.

During February, there was talk of a military coup in Colombia. A group of guerillas, who had been so opposed to the extradition of Colombians to the U.S., were camped out in Pance, the region in the southern part of the city where our school was located. Another school nearby closed when the group was spotted moving closer into the city. Military helicopters flew over the area constantly, trying to keep tabs on their movement, and it became commonplace for me to stop talking when they were flying low because of the noise. Our administration stayed on top of all the activity, and we continued with our work in spite of the efforts of

205

the Anti-American factions to intimidate us. Gradually, the threats subsided, and we dealt with more mundane matters.

Head lice! When Jamie's teacher came down to my room one day to tell me that Jamie had head lice, I was shocked. I had heard about lice spreading quickly among the younger students but didn't know much about it. She gave me all the information I needed, and before long he was lice free. I kept checking my own scalp, and even asked Dan to check for nits, fearful that Jamie may have passed them on to me.

Fortunately, that didn't happen.

His first real act of defiance came one Saturday afternoon when he, Janet, and I were relaxing in the apartment. He was playing with some toy soldiers on the floor in the living room where Janet and I were watching a program on TV. All of a sudden, he got up, walked to the television and changed the channel. Janet and I both looked at him, and I said, "Change it back, Jamie."

He reached for the dial and turned it again to another channel, all the while looking at us with a glare on his face that said, "I'll turn it if I want to."

I got up, walked to the TV, turned it back to the original channel, and said, more forcefully, "Now, Jamie, leave it there. Don't touch it again."

No sooner had I walked back to the sofa and sat down, than he got up and again turned the knob.

"Alright, it's time out. Let's go to your room." He knew about "time out" and usually it worked, but today he rebeled with a vengeance.

He started kicking and screaming "No! No!" When I grabbed his arm, he started swinging. Gradually I was able to get hold of both arms as he arched his back and yelled bloody murder while falling to the floor. This noise went on for several minutes before his tirade turned into heaving sobs. As soon as I could, I picked him up, carried him to his room, and gently placed him on his bed, hoping he would cry himself out. Soon he was just whimpering, and it wasn't long before he closed his eyes. I sat with him a little longer and left only when I was pretty sure the tantrum was over and he was sleeping. It was a cool night, and I pulled the red ruana over him. We talked about the TV later, and I decided to deal with it the same way my mother had handled me when she caught me striking matches under the bed. She sat down with me one day, gave me a book of matches, and told me to strike all I wanted. I struck a few and soon lost interest, of course, and that was the end of the match problem. So, I took Jamie to the television, turned it on, and told him he could choose any channel he wanted and as many as he wanted. He did exactly what I had done and checked out all the channels before indicating he was through and wanted to do something else. We never had problems again with him fiddling with the TV while we were watching, and I hoped I would always have patience to deal with him.

Jamie's teachers said he was absorbing new information like a sponge. He knew his ABCs and was learning his numbers, in English and in Spanish. As he used his crayons, he learned the colors and showed talent and creativity in his drawings. He loved playing with his toy cars and reminded me of my nephews Mike and Travis, who could be totally absorbed in guiding those little machines around the floor and furniture - and people if they happened to be in the way. But his favorite activity was playing with my calculator. With very little instruction from me he learned to add and subtract, delete, turn it on, turn it off, and he even asked about the multiplication and division keys. He also figured out pretty quickly that if the batteries were removed, it wouldn't work. His curiosity about all mechanical things manifested itself when he started taking things apart, such as my alarm clock and other gadgets that could be pried open. When I caught him working on the telephone one day, I was able to stop him just before the earpiece was dismantled. So he was busy and had his share of temper tantrums, but I felt that he was finding his way.

At the end of three weeks, the final adoption papers were not ready, as promised. I stayed on top of everything, but there was nothing I could do to move matters forward. Even Ximena and Nora contacted the judge, who assured them it would all be ready in a couple of weeks. It was time to talk to Marty about my decision, and since he had given me until the end of the month, I couldn't put it off any longer.

I weighed the pros and cons again and now considered some new matters. The adoption fees, Visa and passport applications, a couple of trips Jamie and I would need to take to the Embassy in Bogotá, were all putting a financial strain on me. The need for dollars was increasing, and while I knew my family would never let me go hungry, I didn't want to call on them for anything short of an emergency.

I was also concerned about a job back home. New Bern was the most obvious location at this time because of the condominium and the fact that I had worked there several years, but I had no guarantee I would find a position there that would be a good fit for me. I had been fortunate in my professional life so far, but suppose I found a job in a school that turned out to be less supportive than Colegio Bolivar. How would that affect our lives? My colleagues had been my rock. Having Jamie with me changed everything, and I truly considered him in all decisions.

And the biggest stumbling block of all now was Jamie's Visa. If I was not able to get it by the end of June, when the lease ran out on the apartment and all other support from the school ended, then what? If I resigned, and my position were filled, which would likely be the case by the end of June, there would be no way I could stay in Colombia. Did I dare take a chance on his papers being ready?

There was something inexplicable that drew me back to my family. Even though my immediate family was scattered in New Bern, Whiteville, Myrtle Beach and Wilmington, they would be close enough to visit on a regular basis if I were in New Bern, and, at the time, that was important. I wanted to share my new son with them. And so, I decided to resign a job I loved, in a city I loved, and to leave friends who would remain a part of my life forever. How could I possibly know if I was making the right decision? I finally had to stop agonizing about it and have faith that what I did was the best thing for Jamie and me.

Telling Marty no was difficult. He had offered me a job that inspired me and one that would probably never come around again. He offered me respect as a professional and as a person. But he also understood my decision and offered support. For the remainder of the year, I worked as hard as I ever worked and was determined to let him know the gratitude I felt. When he actually started hiring the new teachers, he asked my opinion and continued to make me feel like a valued part of the school community. What a role model he was.

March 1985

"Look, Mees Woodard, there's your son!" I looked outside my classroom and, galloping across the green expanse between our building and the next building down the hill, was the kinder class, riding their homemade "horses." Whooping and hollering, Jamie was leading the wildly ecstatic posse on their brooms. Each child had made a head for their horse using muslin stuffed with scraps of fabric. Buttons for eyes, brightly colored yarn for the mane, felt pieces for ears and nose, and a smiling mouth with huge buck teeth sketched on with crayons, adorned each head. As quickly as they appeared, they just as quickly disappeared. I was going to miss my open-air classroom just as I knew I would miss my students who knew all about Jamie and adored him. When he brought the "head" home later, I stored it carefully. I was determined to find room for it somewhere in our suitcases when we left for the States.

Patricia and Jamie swimming in Cali, March 1985.

Having decided to return to the States at the end of the school year, I started the countdown to dismantle the apartment and prepare exit papers. My plan was to stay until the end of June since I felt confident that all would be ready by then. Janet and David would be in Cali another year but wanted to rent a house instead of staying in the apartment. They asked for the dining room table and chairs I had bought and other teachers who were staying wanted to buy other things, such as our beds. Getting rid of furniture would be an easy task, and the school would help move the big items when the time came.

I started the paperwork for Jamie's passport and had everything ready except the final adoption papers. When those came through, I could take him downtown and apply for it in Cali since he would be getting a Colombian passport. The Visa was more complicated, but, with Sra. Carvajal's help, I was getting what I needed. In addition to needing the adoption decree, which included the home study, abandonment papers, birth certificate and other statements, all of these had to be translated into English by a registered translator. I decided to make an appointment with the U.S. Embassy in Bogotá to make sure that nothing was being overlooked.

At the end of March, I took a day off from work and made the one-hour flight to Bogotá for my appointment with the official who handled the Visas. I showed him what papers I had, explained where I was in the adoption process, and asked for advice once the papers were granted.

"You seem to have everything in order, but I'm going to give you a list of what you need to bring with you when you return with your son. You'll need extra photos, a statement from a doctor regarding his general physical well-being, and a few other things. Once we have all of those documents, we'll send them to Immigration Services in Panama, and then they will issue the actual visa," he said. It was early in the morning, but he looked and acted tired.

"How long does it usually take to get the visa once everything has been turned in?" I asked.

"It can be anywhere from one to three months," he replied. "Once it all leaves our office, we really don't have any control over the issuance of the visa. It's then in the hands of Immigration personnel."

I did some quick math and figured out that there was a good possibility we could be ready to leave by the end of June. Everything now seemed to depend on getting the adoption papers, and I was determined to doggedly pursue them. I thanked the clerk but didn't feel reassured about the visit. He instilled no confidence that I might get the visa when he said I would, but I knew that if it could be done through my determined efforts, then it would be.

Jamie and I spent the rest of the month involved in our normal activities. On the weekends we went to the club or spent time with the Francos or Platas. When Jamie and I talked about going to the States, he said he wanted to see snow. To him, that's what was in the States. He continued to do well in school and looked forward to being with his classmates and teachers.

When I took him for his medical checkup, the doctor said he was in excellent health and was a bright kid. Jamie played with the stethoscope and tongue depressor and actually had fun in the office. The trip to the dentist was more challenging, especially when fourteen cavities were discovered. We got on a schedule and over the next couple of months gradually took care of the dental problems.

Easter vacation was coming soon, and I was looking forward to having ten days off. Friends invited us to Popayán to see the religious pilgrimage and to take part in all the festivities for *Semana Santa* (Holy Week), but I decided to stay in Cali. There was a lot to do, and I didn't want to be away from the phone too long.

April 1985

On one of our many holidays, Jamie was invited to his first birthday party at the home of one of the teachers. When he told me he didn't know what a birthday party was, I realized how quickly I had forgotten all of the childhood things he had missed. As I explained, he was delighted to find out that people sometimes received gifts. And, yes, that he, too, would have a birthday party in September.

His first overnight trip away from me came during our Easter break to visit a family connected to the school. We had talked about it for a couple of weeks, and he was looking forward to going, until, that is, it was time to go. When the family's driver came to pick him up, he started backing away and looking as if he was going to cry. I called on all of my maternal skills, probably somewhat limited at that time, to reassure him and remind him of all the fun things they were going to do at the finca: go swimming, play with the animals, maybe go horseback riding, and play soccer. Finally, he acquiesced, and as I walked him to the car, he looked sad. But, of course, I was probably the one who looked sad. When he came home the next afternoon, his skin was flushed from a couple of days outside in the sun, and he had had a wonderful time.

On April 16th, I was scheduled to make my final appearance before the judge for the adoption. I was hoping to get the papers that day, but the only thing I got was a verbal declaration that the adoption was approved. I was told that the papers should be ready within a couple of weeks.

April 19 was the tenth anniversary of the M-19 guerilla group, and Marty told us beforehand that school would be canceled that day. The activity from this group tended to come and go in waves, and by mid-April, people who lived in the Pance area, where the groups were camped out, were concerned about the likely uprisings around that date. Security was tight the entire week preceding the 19th, and the number of low-flying helicopters around the school increased dramatically. At 3:00 a.m. Friday morning, Janet and I both woke up to the sounds of gunfire coming from the mountains where confrontations took place frequently. From our apartment on the eighth floor we could see vividly the lights from the explosions and watched the burning of the sugar cane fields. By daylight Friday morning, the four military tanks that Colombia owned were parked in the Plaza de Caycedo in downtown Cali with a reported 60,000 soldiers in the city. The city literally shut down for the day. Jamie, thankfully, slept through all of the noise during the night.

Neighbors and friends we talked to later in the day fully expected the M-19 to move into the city as soon as the troops moved out. My big concern was that the paperwork I needed so desperately, which had to go through the court system, would be slowed down by the disruptions to the point that we wouldn't be able to leave by the end of June.

Ximena made another appeal to the judge who assured her that I would have the papers within fifteen days. If that happened, I could still meet my deadline.

End-of-year activities were beginning at school, and one of the first ones was a dinner honoring the faculty at the restaurant "Cali Viejo," where Mother and I had entertained our friends almost a year earlier. I was able to get a babysitter, and we all enjoyed a terrific evening.

Mother wrote a letter saying that she and Daddy had bought a new house in Whiteville. According to what she said, they wanted to be closer into town, and they needed a smaller yard. I was surprised because she hadn't mentioned it when I saw them over Christmas, but happy if that was what they wanted. I was also a little sad about not being able to return to that house where I had envisioned Jamie playing in the woods among the towering pines and the glorious dogwoods and azaleas in the spring.

The new SAT classes started at the end of April, and with the Self-Study project ending in early May, I was busy. Fortunately, Esmeralda was there to help with the apartment and Jamie. I often reminded myself that when I returned to the States, I wouldn't have that kind of help and knew that I would miss her. She had become a part of our family, and Jamie was especially attached to her.

May 1985

When the SACS visitation team came for their observation on May 8th, we passed with flying colors. The Self-Study was approved, and we were all relieved that no unexpected problems had cropped up. Now we could concentrate on getting through the end of the year classes and exams.

Jamie and I received an invitation to go to Buenaventura, on the Pacific coast, one weekend with the Platas and Francos. I was watching my finances very carefully at this time, but decided we could afford the trip. On the way there we stopped by the roadside to take a swim in a fresh water pool that was fed by a sparkling waterfall. It was beautiful and refreshing and, without my knowing it at first, terrified Jamie. Maybe it was the fact that he was still not swimming on his own, and the rushing water looked threatening. Maybe he thought I was going to let go of him. Or maybe something had happened to him at some other waterfall.

The current was strong but I held him tightly when I sensed that he was getting anxious. When he started screaming, I immediately got him out of the water and did my best to calm him down and didn't even try to get him back in. Eventually everybody got back in the cars, and we drove thirty more minutes to the hotel. To make a long story short, he cried off and on for the entire weekend. We were staying in a nice, comfortable and well-appointed hotel, but I realized that none of that mattered to Jamie. Everything was new, and he was suddenly in an unfamiliar environment. There were also some new people traveling with us, and it was just too much for him. He didn't want anything to do with me and cried every time I approached him. Thankfully, Esteban and Rafael were able to calm him down by talking to him, and by the second night his mood was improving. When we arrived home Sunday night and entered the apartment, he was back to being the Jamie I knew. Later, Ximena reminded me that children were often exasperating and frustrating, and it had nothing to do with me, the parent. That was something I needed to hear at that time.

Finally, on May 16th, the Judge's office called the school and left a message that I could pick up the adoption papers. Thrilled to know that the adoption was now legal and that Jamie truly was my son, I left school as soon as I could and went to his office. I was expecting a friendly smile and congratulations from someone in his office, but the secretary only handed me a manila folder and then the final bill. "You can write a check," she said with a tight smile. So, I wrote a check, handed it to her, thanked her, and walked out of the office. That was it.

By the time I got home, my enthusiasm had returned, and I was grateful that Jamie and Janet and Esmeralda were there. We laughed and I jumped with joy, and Jamie knew that something important concerning his papers had happened. Whatever it was, he knew it meant that we were a little bit closer to getting to the States.

The first appointment I could get at the Embassy in Bogotá was June 5th, the last day of our exams. The clerk I talked to on the phone told me I would need to bring a paper I didn't know about, but one that my lawyer could easily get. My lawyer had not been an easy person to deal with, and I dreaded having to call her again, but I did. She promised she would have the paper ready for me when it was time to go. But the biggest shock was hearing that it could take three more months to get the visa because of delays at Immigration.

"When you arrive here, we'll have to fingerprint you and send copies to the U.S. for a complete FBI investigation. Following that, the results will be sent to Panama or Mexico City for further investigation, and then Immigration Services will issue the visa. All of that is what takes so long."

I was stunned. The very fact that Mexico City was mentioned indicated to me that there was a lot of instability in Panama. Three more months? I couldn't possibly stay three more months in Cali without a job.

"Is there no other recourse?" I asked.

"The only thing that could possibly speed things up would be the intervention of an influential senator or someone who has *palanca,* do you know that word?"

"Yes, absolutely I know that word. Thank you very much for your time. I look forward to seeing you on June 5th," I answered, and started mapping out my strategy for the next few weeks.

The first thing I did was talk to Jamie. He had heard me talk about his papers for a long time, and even though we finally had the adoption papers, he knew we needed others. I told him there was a possibility that we may not be able to go to the States when we hoped, but that we would definitely get there. He seemed okay with that and didn't ask any questions.

Next I talked to Marty and Dr. Ann Hernandez, who was principal of the lower school. She had an adopted child herself and was familiar with the process. She said, "Don't worry. Jamie will be fine. If you have to leave him here for a short time, he will be okay. It will be harder on you than it will be on him. Also, even if he has to return to Chiquitines, it won't be so bad."

I was horrified to think that I might actually have to leave Jamie in Cali, for a week, or for a year. How would he react to that? Would he think I had deserted him? He had been through so much already in his short life that it was devastating to think he may have to face another disappointment. I decided not to talk to him about that possibility yet because there was still a chance that his paperwork would come through.

As soon as I could, I contacted Sra. Carvajal and filled her in on the latest news regarding the Visa.

"Yes, Patricia. That is very common. I understand about your maybe having to leave without Jamie, and if he needs to stay here for a while longer, he can," she said.

"If that should happen, I will certainly make a contribution to the orphanage for his care. Right now, I still haven't given up hope that we'll be able to leave together," I replied.

"Tranquila, Patricia. Don't worry."

I was overwhelmed with gratitude but becoming more and more concerned that I was not being realistic. I finally acknowledged that it would take a miracle at this point to get everything in order for a June departure and accepted that that was not likely to happen.

In early May, the import teachers were instructed to have their household items ready to ship out by the end of the month. I was sorting our things and making packing lists that had to be included in the boxes. I made a separate pile of clothes and toys for Jamie in case he stayed behind for a while, and the apartment was looking bare. We kept a few kitchen items, and whatever Janet decided not to take with her I was going to leave for Ximena.

Early one morning, Jamie and I went to the government building downtown to apply for his passport. This was supposed to be a much easier process than getting the Visa but Dr. Hernandez at school had told me to be there by 6:00 a.m. Apparently, the doors to the building were open for only thirty minutes, and if you didn't get inside during that time, you were out of luck that day.

The first day, we didn't get inside. I learned quickly that if we wanted to get in, we'd have to run as fast as we could across the plaza when the signal to enter was given. We could then expect to wait a few hours in line before we could actually fill out the papers. On the second day, trying to prepare Jamie, I told him to stay close by and, when I gave him a signal, to run as fast as he had ever run. There were no orderly lines outside where we waited, so everybody was jostling about waiting for the bell to ring. When it was almost time to go in, I glanced to my side and saw Jamie chasing the pigeons across the plaza. I yelled his name and motioned for him to "COME HERE! NOW!" He heard me, and this time, we made it inside just at the last moment.

I've always thought that that day was the day I came as close to being a Colombian as I ever would. Once inside, we stood in line and waited and watched the line move slowly. As we got closer and closer to the window, I noticed that groups of nicely dressed people, obviously upper class, would enter the room and walk up to a person in line, speak to them and step in line. The lone person would then leave. After watching this happen a few times, I realized that people were paying someone to hold a place in line for them.

I nearly went ballistic when I saw it happen because I knew the lines would close at a certain time, and even though we were in the building, we may not get to the window, which would mean another trip down here tomorrow. Finally, in my best (worst?) Spanish, I asked, "What is going on? This is my second day here, and if people continue to break in line, I may never get to the window! I have a child with me who needs his passport! Please, don't do this!"

I could hear words of support coming from the people in line, and I felt as if I were at a political rally, being cheered by the crowd for a speech that expressed their feelings. Immediately, the latest group of interlopers politely stepped aside and let us move to the head of the line. "Thank you," I said forcefully and silently dared any of them to challenge me. My connection to the people was secure and I felt like one of them. We made the application without further incident and were on our way home soon.

Senior exams started at the end of May, and graduation was scheduled for June 7th. With each passing day I recognized that the time for deciding my next step was here. My biggest concern was planning what I would say to Jamie if I found out on our trip to Bogotá on June 5th that his papers could not possibly be ready in time for us to leave together. So, before the trip I started saying things like, "I may have to leave before you, but I'll be back soon to get you." "Sra. Carvajal said she would love to have you stay with her a little while." Anything I could think of to lessen the blow. He never responded much when I said those things because I'm sure he had no concept of what they meant. We continued to go to school and the club and visit with friends. I tried to keep our lives as normal as possible.

June 1985

Finally, early on June 5th, we took a cab to the airport for the trip to Bogotá. Jamie never wore long pants in Cali, but I thought they would be appropriate for the cooler temperatures in the capital, and he was excited about being dressed up. Also, this would be his first flight, and I was praying he wouldn't get sick but decided against giving him Dramamine since it was a short flight.

He was a good little traveler and had no problems on the plane. During the cab ride to the embassy, I was in a surprisingly reflective mood. Had it really been nine years since I lived and worked in Bogotá? The route we were taking through the city was not familiar, and I wondered if it had changed that much, or were we just in an area I didn't know. Were we close to the school? Or our old apartment? I thought about Dot and Jerry and other friends and wondered where they were and what they were doing. Before I had a chance to get sentimental, we arrived at the embassy on a glorious, cool, and sunny morning.

Jamie was always excited about these trips, and after asking directions and then checking in at the appropriate office, we returned outside where he immediately set about exploring the grounds. Those of us who had business at the embassy usually waited many hours, and thanks to someone's foresight, the bathrooms and waiting areas were located outside the main building. There was a refreshment stand where Jamie asked for a cup of juice, and I ordered a *tinto*. We sat down on benches, and as soon as Jamie finished, he wanted to run around the well-tended garden. I reminded him not to pick the flowers, just to look and smell, and to let me know if he needed to use the bathroom. Under no circumstances was he to enter the bathroom alone. I watched him carefully and glanced through the papers I had, as if by checking them one more time, nothing would be lacking.

Shortly, he bounded back to where I was sitting and said he needed to use the bathroom – now! We walked to the building: apparently males and females used the same one, and passed a young Colombian woman and child coming out. We nodded, and Jamie and I walked in. The room was large and airy with cool tiled floors, and sunshine was pouring in through many large, open, unscreened windows. There were several stalls on the left with short doors that provided only a modicum of privacy. An L-shaped room, the back part opened to the left.

Since Jamie was already struggling to get his new pants down, I didn't notice the urinals in the back part of the room. I ushered him into the first stall while frantically trying to release his stuck zipper and wondered what I would do if he had an accident. It had never occurred to me to bring extra clothes. But not to worry. He finally got settled and suddenly, I heard footsteps coming into the room. There was no mistaking that this was not the sound of the high-heeled shoes most Colombian women wore. The clomp of heavy boots continued the length of the room and stopped at the same time Jamie said, "Okay, let's go – I'm through!" Not knowing if we should nonchalantly walk out then or wait for HIM (it had to be a man) to leave was a matter quickly settled when Jamie opened the door, jumped out, and headed for the sinks. As his mother, I had to follow, right?

Standing at the back of the room in front of a urinal was a well-dressed man, at least from my view, in that time-honored stance that makes all men look armless from the back. He didn't even glance over his shoulder as Jamie washed his hands and, as usual, splashed water everywhere. Just as he was finishing, our surprise visitor turned around and adjusted his clothes. He looked at us indulgently, in that kind, gentle way Colombian men tend to regard women and children, shrugged his shoulders gracefully and passed out of our lives. I was rather shocked to have shared a bathroom with a strange man and chalked up that experience to cultural differences. When we walked back outside, I had to smile when I thought about the many times I had stood in line at public events, waiting to use the women's bathroom, only to see men walk in and out of theirs with no waiting. Maybe the Colombians were on to something here.

Jamie's energy and enthusiasm could bring a smile to my face at the least expected time, and today was a day I had not expected to do much smiling. As we left the bathroom, I gave him a hug and a big smile, and we went back to our waiting.

When we finally met for our appointment, my worst fears were confirmed when the official told me it would probably be three months before the Visa would be issued. The embassy would send the papers to Immigration, and they would contact me if anything was missing. He apologized, saying that the U.S. citizens the embassy was there to serve, often were the last ones to be helped. He also mentioned the political situation in Panama, indicating that what happened at U.S. Immigration Services in Panama would certainly affect how quickly my request could be processed. Even though I had been vetted by the FBI when I moved to Cali a year and a half ago, I would need to be fingerprinted again and go through the same investigation once more. Before leaving, Jamie and I walked to a room where I was fingerprinted, and, curious as ever, he asked if he could also be fingerprinted. "Later," I told him.

It was somewhat of a relief to know now where we were headed. I talked to Jamie about what I knew we had to do - separate for a while - and he just didn't react much. I told him I would write and that some of the people at Chiquitines would read my letters to him. Colleagues from school had volunteered to visit him if needed. I also reassured him that he would have enough to eat, and when school started next September, if we still didn't have the papers, then he could continue at another school until I could come back for him. I did everything I could to let him know that I loved him and would never desert him. I was his mom forever.

Graduation was on June 7th, and then we had a holiday before wrapping up the year at school on June 14. My friends and colleagues stayed close by those last two weeks, and some even postponed their own vacations to be with me and help in any way they could.

On Wednesday, June 25th, with the apartment emptied except for the things I was packing in my suitcase, I took Jamie back to Chiquitines. He tried to put up a strong front, but I was his Mom, and I knew he was upset. We talked and sat on the swings, and I took some pictures of him. I also gave him a picture of the two of us together. I reminded him how much I loved him and that I would be back as soon as I could. I tried to keep the tone light, and when it was finally time to leave, I walked him inside to Sra.'s office and gave him one last hug and kiss. He held on a little longer than he usually did, and then he spirited himself away. Drained, I spoke to Sra. Carvajal a few more minutes and then left to return to the empty apartment.

I stopped at the grocery store on the way home and picked up some empanadas and *pan de bono* and then spent a busy night doing my final packing. Esmeralda was coming in the next day to help with a few chores in the apartment, and I planned to give her any food that was left. Also, I knew there would be toiletry items and towels to leave behind, and she always seemed glad to get those things. My suitcase was jam-packed, and I started pulling things out so I could take the most important things. The one thing I regretted most not being able to take with me was the musical score for "South Pacific," which John had given me when the play was over. There was just no way that one more thing would fit in that suitcase.

The next day was a continuation of the packing and getting things organized for the landlord. When Esmeralda came in, we both worked until late in the afternoon. I told her to take whatever she wanted and then gave her an extra two weeks' pay, which was customary when a maid's job was terminated. We said a tearful goodbye, and I extended my best wishes. She was considering taking a class to help her get a job as a secretary, and I encouraged her to try. She was smart, and I knew she could succeed if she just had an opportunity.

On my last night in Cali, I stretched out on the carpet, placed some clothes behind my head for a pillow, and pulled more clothes over me for a blanket. I tried not to think too much about Jamie and the last eighteen months because I didn't want to be melancholy, and I needed my energy to plan my next steps. There would be plenty of time for reflections later. Right now, I had to get home, get a job, and call everybody I knew who could help with the visa. Gratefully, sleep came easily that night.

Friday morning, at the time of day that was usually so sunny and sparkling, clouds rolled in. Rafael arrived at 6:30 a.m. and helped carry my overweight luggage to the car. Always charming and elegant, he joked about how much I was taking back to the States and asked if I was smuggling out Colombian artifacts. I could always depend on Rafael to keep the proper perspective. After many years of exposure to the Colombian culture, I had come to appreciate their strength and bravery and knew there would be no tears today. Passionate feelings and soaring spirits, yes! But no tears, and I was grateful.

After checking in at the airport, Rafael and I shared a cup of *tinto* and talked about the weather and nothing in particular. He left me with a hilarious joke about an armadillo so that when it was time for my departure, I was still laughing. As we said "goodbye" and "see you soon," I walked through the door and waved one last time.

Mission Accomplished

On June 5, 1985, the US Embassy in Bogotá filed the petition for approval of Jamie's immigrant visa. On May 5, 1986, exactly eleven months later, the petition was approved, and I was notified on May 7. Through the efforts of my uncle Harry and his letters to Senators Strom Thurmond of South Carolina and Jesse Helms of North Carolina, I was finally able to bring Jamie home. Misunderstandings, language barriers, questionable practices, and the relocation of Immigration offices in Panama - all contributed to the delay.

Do I regret having faith in the system and believing that our best interests would be a top priority? Not a chance. Do I regret resigning from Colegio Bolivar at the time I did and not heeding Marty's advice about the possible delays? Absolutely. But even staying another year, I realized, would not have guaranteed a different outcome regarding the visa although it would have guaranteed that we would have been together. What mattered now was that Jamie and I made it through a challenging ordeal and survived as a family.

After a quick return trip to Colombia with two days in Cali and two more days in Bogotá finalizing the last bureaucratic requirements, we headed to El Dorado airport for our flight home. When we passed through Immigration, with every document ever connected to Jamie's visa in my carry-on, I was on edge. I knew how easy it would be for someone to indicate that something was not in order, and we'd be stranded again. But sometimes, things go the way they should, and once our papers were examined and approved, we were ushered to another waiting room, which must have been set aside for special passengers. It was a small room, with comfortable chairs, coffee and juice on a serving table, a spectacular view of the airplanes coming and going across a backdrop of the majestic Andes, and a guard at the door (this time a smiling guard). We sat down to wait for our call to board.

Soon, a lively, dark-skinned maid came into the room and spoke to us in a friendly manner. She poured me a cup of coffee and gave Jamie a cup of juice. As she bantered with him, he relaxed. She asked where we were going, and Jamie said "North Carolina," while smiling and flashing his adorable dimple. I noticed she was wearing a rather long skirt that swirled as she turned, and her hair was piled on top of her head. When she handed us fruit from a large basket, a vision flashed in my mind of another Colombian woman, who appeared in my consciousness years ago, walking down a sunny, narrow path with a basket of fruit on her head, and coffee bushes and banana trees shading her trail. Here she was! She *did* exist, and she was here now to let us know that everything was going to be okay.

"Come," she seemed to say, *"It's time. There are more adventures, more friends, more expressions of love waiting for you. Go home now."* And so we did.

Epilogue

Bogotá
February 19, 2009...

My former roommate Dot and I are riding in a car in Bogotá with the Director of Colegio Nueva Granada's driver, Jose. We've been in the city a couple of days and are now on our way to the school for a visit, many years after we taught there. As we drive through the streets on a cool, sunny morning, so typical of the good weather days in Bogotá, nothing but the weather is familiar. I recognize no landmarks on the way up the mountain, except the view of the Andes in the distance. What used to be a winding mountain road that even taxis were hesitant to maneuver, is now a bustling, four-lane highway passing directly in front of the gates to the school. Buses, taxis, and cars vie for space, and condominiums and office buildings surround the campus. Certainly no young boys carry cardboard and newspapers on their skateboards, zipping around the hills in this area today. The city I knew of five million people in 1975 is now approaching a population of nine million, and I wonder if I'll be able to accomplish my goal on this trip. I'm looking for inspiration and a little kick to start the memoir.

When I retired from teaching in North Carolina in 2004, one of my projects was to finally write a memoir about my year in Bogotá. I had started it many years earlier when I was thinking about the need to leave a record of my experience in Colombia for my son, Jamie. I thought it was important for him to know something about his heritage other than what he heard on the news and read in the newspapers, and I wanted very much to help him preserve his cultural identity. So I thought that putting down on paper what I remembered from my time in Colombia would help me achieve that goal.

Fortunately, my parents had saved the letters I wrote to them during those years, so I felt like I had a head start. With a full-time job (plus a part-time job occasionally), parenting, graduate school, and aging parents who deserved my time, however, the hours I needed to work on a manuscript just weren't there. The years passed by with no first draft, and then, on April 1, 2001, the unthinkable happened. My adorable, funny, loving and challenging son became a homicide victim. With a single gunshot, my life, as I knew it, shattered, and my twenty-three-year old son was no more. Time, and support from friends and family, helped me climb out of my hole of shock and despair, and gradually my life took on meaning again.

I read the letters from Bogotá many times, but couldn't bring myself to read the ones from Cali, where I adopted Jamie. So that was how I started with the project: thinking about Bogotá because by then, I was sure I wouldn't write about Cali. I felt as if I had enough information to leave my nieces and nephews and other family members a record of a dream I once had, and that was one of the objectives: to leave a record for them. Perhaps one day they would enjoy reading about it, or maybe be inspired to pursue their own dreams. Regardless, it was important to me to examine my feelings about Colombia and come to terms with my attachment to the people and the country and the way it always caressed my soul.

Through the internet, I had stayed in touch with my Colombian friends and had even found Dot, who had settled in Phoenix with her daughter Luci, married now and the mother of two. As I gathered my thoughts and letters for the memoir, I realized that what was missing was the memories that someone else who was there might have, which weren't mentioned in the letters to my parents – and surely there were many things I didn't put in the letters. I needed some help jogging my memory! In the fall of 2008, Dot and I had not seen each other since 1977 in the Dominican

Republic. With a few e-mails and phone calls, she agreed to a return trip to Bogotá and then a visit with my friends in Cali, and finally, a trip to Cartagena where she had taught for a year. This was exactly what I needed, and I knew she would be the perfect companion. My only regret was that I couldn't find Jerry.

We met at the airport in Miami on the evening of February 16, 2009, before our flight to Bogotá early the next morning. After thirty two years we had no trouble recognizing each other and dove right into talking about our time at Colegio Nueva Granada. For the next nine days, she shared her memories, I shared mine, and we laughed at how different they sometimes were. For example, she didn't remember my boyfriend Paul at all, and then I remembered that he and I always went to Melgar or some other place usually with his friends while Dot was taking care of her daughter.

I had contacted the school before our arrival and was steered to the office of Alumni Affairs whose Director was Adriana Perez, a former student at CNG. She had already spoken to Isabella Delgado, the Director's assistant, whom Dot and I both remembered, and she made arrangements for us to be picked up at the hotel by Dr. McComb's driver. We found out that Charlotte Samper, a guidance counselor who was the daughter of Dr. Samper, the staff physician when we were there, was still working at the school; also, Gustavo Vega, a math teacher, whom we both knew, had spent his entire career at CNG and was thinking about retirement.

As Jose pulled into the gated driveway at school and waited for the guards to let us in, I eagerly looked around, hoping to recapture a sense of something familiar. The campus was barely recognizable. Through an impressive brick entry, new buildings spilled in all directions, but the blooming flowers and lush foliage, which still defined the grounds, were the only things that stirred a feeling of identity. Dot commented on the Eucalyptus trees outside her former classroom, but I had no memory of them. The main entrance into the administration area hadn't changed much, but the parking area had been moved. And the buses! When did they get this modern fleet of futuristic vehicles? We surmised that the seats were cushioned, and there were probably bathrooms on board, maybe even a heater. With tinted windows, we speculated they were bullet-proof, as well.

Adriana graciously welcomed us and we visited with Isabella, Charlotte and even stopped by Gustavo's classroom to say hello. Our old classrooms were just as they were when we were there, except the old blackboards with the felt erasers had been replaced with the new dry-erasable ones. It was not hard to imagine that we had slipped back in time and that we were once again busy young teachers, working on lesson plans, waiting for the weekend to come so we could explore the city. The import teachers we met that day could easily have been there when we were there, and I felt an immediate bond with them. Dot and I wondered if they could see themselves in us as we talked to them about their experiences in Bogotá and explained why we were there.

After lunch in the new cafeteria, Adriana asked if we would mind being interviewed on tape for a book she was compiling on memories of CNG by alumni. We were happy to help out and had fun talking about what we had brought to CNG as individual teachers. A theme quickly developed around individualized instruction, and we both realized, perhaps for the first time, that our efforts were still embedded in the curriculum at CNG. I had nearly forgotten about all the work and effort that we had put into identifying the needs of our students and then choosing appropriate activities for them. Adriana thanked us, on tape, and acknowledged our contributions to the high quality and standards of the CNG community.

After a worthwhile day I came away from the visit with respect and admiration for the entire school. Providing for the child, encouraging excellence, leadership, scholarship and character remained the guiding principles of the school's vision. A new area of emphasis, service, had been implemented, and I was thrilled to know that these privileged young people were now giving back to the community in many ways. CNG itself had built a small separate school for underprivileged children and supported it with donations from the CNG families and alumni. Several times I was tempted to ask if they needed any math teachers.

We noticed the delightful weather in Bogotá, especially since it had always been an issue. Even on the school campus the frigid wind didn't seem to blow as hard as I remembered. Someone told us that global warming had taken place there, just like everywhere, and while there was still plenty of rain and temperatures were cool, we didn't need our heavy turtleneck sweaters. Very few people wore ruanas, and I regretted that, because that one article of clothing defined one of my most vivid, visual memories of the city. We found out that CNG is in the western part of the city, not the northern part, as we had both thought.

When Dot and I explored a new upscale mall in *la zona g,* we weren't surprised at all to see armed guards at the entrance and especially in the area of the ATMs. We shook our heads in amazement that we were able to get money from a machine in public and, at the same time, felt grateful that the guards were there. Safety was still an issue in Bogotá, and we instinctively kept a low profile. I was hoping to find the restaurant *Casa Vieja* where I had first eaten *ajiaco* and was disappointed to find out that the city now had three *Casas Viejas.* I didn't have a clue how to find the one where Paul had told me about the man who was assassinated leaving the restaurant, so we had lunch at one that was close to the shopping center. The ajiaco was just as delectable as I remembered, and we lingered over our meal and attentive service.

Dot and Patricia enjoying *ajiaco* at Casa
Vieja, Bogotá, February 2009.

Dot and I hired a driver at our hotel to take us around the city one day, and he told us how it had changed. Chía, the little pueblo we used to visit about an hour from the city, was now a suburb of Bogotá with a major highway connecting the two. Melgar, the quiet, secluded, weekend getaway at the bottom of a curving mountain road, where I spent so many weekends in the sun, had become a sprawling tourist mecca. A lot of land there had been cleared for new hotels and restaurants, and I thought about the jungle I used to stare at from the pool of our cabins.

We rode around the neighborhood of our old apartment, but the building was gone; in its place, another nondescript structure. Diego, our driver, pointed out the building where DAS, the scary and mysterious government organization where we sat on the floor smoking cigarettes and drinking coffee on a cold, dreary day many years ago, is located. He also pointed out the American Embassy, where I had spent several difficult days trying to get Jamie's visa about twenty-five years earlier. None of it was familiar. Demonstrations were going on at the time we passed in the car, and Diego said, "It's normal." I was curious to know if Oma's, the outdoor restaurant on the fashionable *avenida quince,* where Paul and I spent many late nights with friends over coffee and cognac, was still there, but we couldn't find it.

Only once did we see a donkey and wagon on a major street. We visited the old part of town where I was hoping to find the co-ops where we used to buy the local handicrafts, but only found stores selling touristy items. I told myself authentic handicrafts had to be there somewhere, and if only I had more time, I'd find them. We revisited the Gold Museum, Simon Bolívar's home, and saw the Botero Museum for the first time. We could still buy empanadas and fruits from kioskos on the streets, and people continued to move briskly as they went about their business – and nearly all seemed to be talking on cell phones. I remembered spending weeks without phone service when we lived there and couldn't imagine having access to the technology available in Colombia now.

Cali
February 20, 2009...

After a few days in the capital, Dot and I headed to Cali where I was looking forward to seeing my friends and visiting Colegio Bolivar. Many changes had taken place in my Colombian families. Ximena, Rafael, and Margarita had been in a serious car accident in 1993, and Ximena and Rafael were hospitalized for several months. Margarita, the least injured, and their other daughter, Maria Isabel, helped care for them during their recuperation. While we had stayed in touch over the years, I hadn't seen any of them except Ximena's daughter, Margarita, who had spent six weeks with me in New Bern during the summer of 1996.

Maria Isabel, their older daughter, was a physical therapist now, married to an orthopedic surgeon. Together they opened their own treatment centers and expanded into several locations in the city. They had two sons. Margarita was recently married and had one daughter. They stayed strong as a family.

Unfortunately, Rafael's import business had suffered during the years along with the economy in Colombia, and times had been hard for them. They had lost nearly all of their material possessions. Ximena had taken many jobs to help support her family, and her faith and optimism sustained them while they waited for conditions to improve. Nora, Ximena and Esteban's mother, and Cilla, their aunt, had recently passed away. So, it was a period of much personal upheaval.

Since my last visit in 1986, Esteban and Marta's daughter, Isabel, had grown up and was in her last year at the University. Soon she would be Dr. Isabel Plata, doctor of psychology. They had also been blessed with a second daughter, Sofía, who was now ten years old. Esteban was still in the pizza business, supplying schools with daily pizzas, and had opened a restaurant and motel at Lake Calima where they had finally built their vacation home overlooking the lake. Most touchingly, Marta had survived breast cancer and had recently finished chemotherapy treatments. Her prognosis was excellent, and, when we arrived, she was gradually getting back her strength and hair.

But one thing had improved for all of them. Nearly everybody now had washing machines, which, in many cases, eliminated the need for live-in maids. The many young girls and women who, in the past, were destined to a life of domestic work, were now looking for opportunities in other areas. The economy was changing, and with presidential elections coming in a year, there was a sense of optimism.

Without a thought about themselves and any misfortunes they may have experienced, my Colombian family welcomed me back with love and open arms. Of course, they knew about Jamie's death and spoke freely and openly about him. Their approach was good for me, and I was encouraged to say anything I wanted. They asked a lot of questions but never passed judgment on my decisions. I was always amazed at the way we were able to communicate with our limited language skills, but we did. Their support was solid, and I was happy to be with them.

Their generosity extended to being our driver and tour guide during the next few days, and our first trip was to Colegio Bolivar with Esteban and Isabel, called Isa. It seemed impossible that nearly twenty five years had passed since I eagerly embraced an eighteen-month experience that would have such an impact on my life. As we approached the school, I noticed the traffic. The Blanco y Negro buses, upon which I had relied heavily, looked tired and worn out. A new transit system, called *el Mío,* was scheduled to start operating within days. Once through the security gate, we headed to the office of Carolina Chavez, Alumni Director. I marveled that the campus grounds were as green and lush as ever, and how the relentless heat seemed to magically disappear when we stepped in the shade. The new buildings looked as if they had always been there.

The auditorium where I spent so much time in the Spring of 1984 seemed to resonate with the sounds I remembered from "South Pacific," and I could clearly see and hear "Bloody Mary" and "Some Enchanted Evening" being performed.

The new outdoor eating area reminded me of a room upstairs for faculty and staff breaks and where they gave me the shower for Jamie. I remembered the students lounging on the grass during lunchtime, eating empanadas and a strange kind of hot dog that had cheese inside, usually followed by a quick siesta.

As we walked to the pool area I thought about how impressed I was when I first saw it. Having access to a pool like that on a daily basis was thrilling, and I made use of it frequently – especially on the weekends when we were allowed on campus. It's where I took Jamie the first day we went out together.

The soccer field was just as I remembered, except on this day there were no students playing a match. Yet, I can still see them in my mind, charging up and down the field with the fans cheering from the sidelines.

The new state-of-the-art library and computer center, called the Martin Felton Center, took my breath away. In 1984, if I remember correctly, one classroom had a few computers, which were, I think, TRS-80s. There was no actual computer class then, but Russell Bloom's voice still echoed in my memory as the electricity flickered and computer screens died. In those early days of experimentation some brave souls took on the task of moving the school into a computer-savvy environment. Now, in 2009, it was obvious they had achieved it.

In my old classroom, I experienced again the unique sensation of teaching in a room with three walls and a panoramic view of Colombia at its best: the snow-capped mountains of Nevado del Ruiz in the distance, the grass that still made me want to go barefooted, and the students who brought so much joy to my life. They were focused, intelligent, friendly, curious, lively and could they ever dance! I remember the day one of them said, "Mees Woodard, look, there's your son!" And there his class was, romping across the lawn with their homemade broom "horses."

I caught a glimpse of Alain Bouchard and even spoke briefly with Manuelita Velasco, both teachers when I was there. Dr. Felton had retired, but was living in Cali, and I was delighted to meet his daughter who was now teaching in the kinder program.

We ended our tour of the school with Carolina, who helped me recall some precious memories as I witnessed the new exciting times unfolding. My life had definitely been enriched by being a part of Colegio Bolivar, and I was greatly moved by revisiting a very special time in my life.

Before leaving, Carolina said, "Patricia, we're planning a big reunion June 12, 2010, for the alumni. Why don't you come?"

I hadn't thought about returning to Cali so soon, but thought, "Why not?"

"Thank you, Carolina. Keep me posted. I'd love to come back."

For the next few days, my friends entertained us. I had hoped to return to Sylvia, where the Indians in their purple and pink ruanas lived, but it was considered too dangerous to travel in that area. We went to Lake Calima for the weekend and stayed in Esteban and Marta's home overlooking the lake. When I asked if they ever went to river now they replied, "Rarely ever. This is where we come on the weekends. For us, it is a blessing." The house was right beside Esteban's restaurant and cabins, which his brother Nacho took care of during the week. At the lake we also went by Maria Isabel's vacation house, called *la casa azul,* the blue house, painted a vibrant shade of blue reminiscent of Freda Kahlo's blue house in Mexico. We had wine and cheese before a boat ride with Esteban's brother Ismael and his wife, Patty. At night we rode into a little town, Darien, and walked around the square and ate *arepas.* Sleep came easily on those cool nights.

Back in Cali, Dot and I and various family members visited the new zoo, went shopping, and rode by my former apartment building, *Las Torres de Santiago de Cali.* Xavier joined us for a trip to a new mall, *Chipichapi,* and he and Esteban followed us at a discreet but protective distance as we walked from store to store. We ate papayas, mangos, empanadas and had lunch one day at an Italian restaurant, Salerno's. One afternoon, Maria Isabel drove us to her elegant apartment for coffee. At 5:00 p.m. during the week, environmental conservation measures go into effect, which limit the number of cars driving in the city. One's license number determines what nights people can drive. On this night Ma. Isabel had to park her car at 5:00 p.m., so we walked back to our nearby hotel along *el río Cauca.* On this beautiful evening, even though the crime rate in Cali was still high, I felt safe on these streets.

Dot, who had never met my friends in Cali, was blown away by their hospitality and generosity. Since she was my friend, she was automatically their friend. She commented on how different her life would have been in Colombia if she had had Colombian friends like these. I acknowledged that truth, and counted my blessings.

On our last day, Esteban drove us to the airport. We were saying goodbye, thank you, and doing a lot of hugging while promising to send pictures soon. Suddenly, Esteban said, "Patricia, we *luf* you! Come back soon!"

"I love you, too! And I'll be back!" Yes, I thought, there's still a lot to do here.

Cartagena
February 25, 2009…

Our last stop was Cartagena, and by the time Dot and I arrived, we were both tired of living out of a suitcase. In this beautiful, historic city on the coast, I had to make a real effort to get out since all I could think about was getting home and working on the memoir. We hired a driver to take us to the school where Dot taught before she went to Bogotá. The only person she found from that time was her former landlady. After a short visit with her, we saw what we could, trying to avoid the hot, humid, and tropical oppression during the middle of the day. People disappeared from the streets at mid day but came out aggressively when the balmy afternoon winds picked up. An international film festival was going on, so a lot of tourists were walking around town, eating in the restaurants, and taking the horse and buggy rides through the downtown area. Several times on the narrow sidewalks I nearly stepped in mierna and decided I needed to come back to Cartagena when I was in a better frame of mind. The most thrilling part of that layover for me was seeing Gabriel García Márquez' vacation house. His book *One Hundred Years of Solitude* still resonated in my consciousness, and I thought about the day in 1975 when I was flying to Colombia for the first time, reading his magical story. Each time I re-read it in the following years, I knew I had touched on something spiritual.

My objective on this trip had been to jog my memory back into the mind set I'd had nearly thirty-five years earlier. I had hoped that spending time with Dot in Bogotá, revisiting the school and the city, recalling those times would give me the insight and inspiration to pursue my memoir. And also, I wanted to visit Cali and my friends there, to see if I should think about returning permanently. Did I meet those objectives? Absolutely! I was eager to write and, yes, Cali was calling. Could there be a third time?

Printed in the United States
by Baker & Taylor Publisher Services